HORSE BRASSES

and other small items for the collector

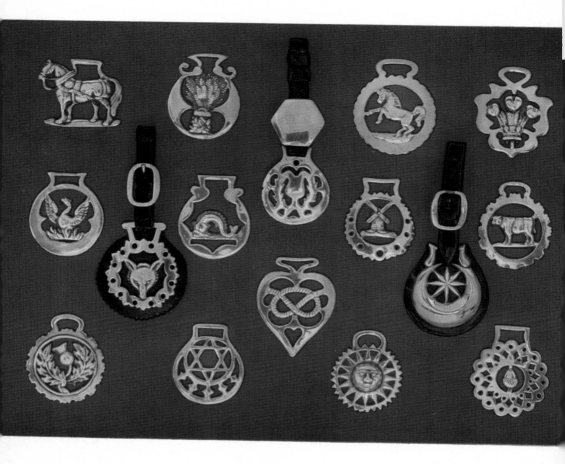

HORSE BRASSES

FROM THE COLLECTION OF MRS W. BURNARD PHILLIPS

Of the sixteen examples four—the horse (top left), the cow (right middle), the Staffordshire knot (lower centre) and the sun (bottom line, third from left)— are souvenir brasses. In his first chapter Bernard Hughes describes how souvenirs can be distinguished from genuine brasses.

HORSE BRASSES

and other small items for the collector

BY

G. BERNARD HUGHES

COUNTRY LIFE LIMITED LONDON

Published in 1956
by Country Life Limited
Tavistock Street London W.C.2
Printed in Great Britain by
Lowe & Brydone (Printers) Ltd
London
Third impression 1964

Contents

Illustrations

Preface

ONE of the major delights and privileges of writing about antiques, I have found, is the way in which fellow enthusiasts approach me, sharing their experiences and inviting me to examine their cabinets. Occasionally this has enabled me to establish facts of technique of far wider application than the matter in hand, such as some details revealed by the unique Chubb collection of loving cups (Chapter Eight). And more than once it has prompted me to probe some fascinating byway and establish the facts behind the commonly accepted curio sales-talk—facts that are often far more interesting and revealing than the oft-repeated tale.

To me, and apparently to many of my readers, much of the joy in studying an antique lies in the way it reflects the life of the period and people who produced it. This includes, of course, the social life and customs, such as produced, for example, the extra-ordinarily efficient little baluster wine measure (Chapter Six) and the elaborate paraphernalia of the snuff-taker (Chapter Three). But to me it must also include various aspects of technique and crafts-manship, and this is where a wide knowledge of past materials and methods has aided me in sifting precious facts from often ludicrous fiction. In these days, my correspondence proves, other collectors too enjoy their treasures fully only when they fully understand them.

Even familiar horse brasses, twinkling companionably beside the hearth, have a story to tell when the changes in the colour and texture of their metal can demonstrate changes in brass manu-facturing techniques.

In this book I have deliberately concentrated on byways where I have found the truth refreshingly different from the customary fiction. Moreover, they include a number of subjects where there is a very real threat that reproductions and fakes will become so widely accepted as genuine, but scarcely worth collecting, that the original may be passed over by those who could best appreciate its distinctive beauty of design and craftsmanship.

As in my previous volumes on *Collecting Antiques* and *More About Collecting Antiques*, each chapter represents a serious effort to present factual information without becoming tiresomely tech-nical. But each chapter represents, too, many happy hours shared

9

with people whose understanding, interest and enthusiasm are the surest guarantee that our country's great heritage of craftsmanship will not be forgotten. To them I offer appreciative thanks, and also, as ever, to Mr Frank Whitaker, Editor of *Country Life*, in whose pages I first met so many of these friends.

1956   G. BERNARD HUGHES

CHAPTER ONE

Horse Brasses

HORSE brasses in England have a two-thousand-year history, although this name for the familiar and wholly delightful pieces of Victorian 'harness furniture' is less than a century old. The Roman occupiers of Britain (A.D. 50 to A.D. 410) introduced the custom of enriching the leather harness of driven horses with bronze amulets. These were looped disks of highly polished bronze raised in the centre with a low boss and sometimes encircled with three to five folds. These amulets, supposed to represent the sun god, guardian of driven horses, closely resembled modern horse brasses. Three pairs, with considerably worn loops, unearthed with other bronze horse trappings in North Wales during 1868, were described in *Archaeologia* of that year by Sir Wollaston Franks. Others were excavated at Caerleon in Wales early this century.

Romans and Britons alike believed that such amulets would ward off the evil eye. Highly polished protective amulets, flickering with every movement of the horse, distracted the evil eye and so destroyed its power. Since it was supposed to inflict its greatest harm when the horse was displayed in triumph, horse brasses were worn on festival and ceremonial occasions, a custom continued to modern times at horse shows and fairs.

Ceremonial occasions at later periods in England saw horse trappings bedecked with as many as two dozen flat bronze amulets, all exactly alike and highly polished. Normally a driven horse wore no more than a single amulet, for bronze was an expensive metal. A fourteenth-century illuminated manuscript in the British Museum shows a mounted knight, the harness of his horse carrying fifteen flat heart-shaped amulets which might be in gold, gilded silver, bronze, or possibly latten. Engravings of the late seventeenth century illustrate gaily caparisoned carriage horses wearing amulets of gilded silver in shapes including the sun, crescent, heart, and fleur-de-lys. Up to this time the amulets were suspended from a leather harness strap extending horizontally from the martingale around the haunches and to the front again.

In the Georgian period it became customary to suspend a single brass, known as a face-piece, upon the forehead of a driven horse. This often took the form of a sun-flash, composed of a brass disk, its centre raised into a high dome encircled with a wide flat rim, the edge sometimes serrated after 1820. In some mid-Victorian examples the flat rim was pierced with twelve triangular rays extending outwards to the serrated edge. Later the rim might be encircled with drilled perforations; from about 1880 the whole brass including dome and perforations was stamped.

The sunflash of the eighteenth century was hand-shaped from thick latten plate, extended almost across the horse's face, and weighed about six ounces. When burnished these brasses radiated beams of light in the sunshine and scintillated with the horse's every movement. Sun-flashes were particularly common in Kent. There is no evidence, however, that they were intended to serve more than an ornamental purpose, although in a day when the power of the evil eye was still a lively superstition it would have been considered an effective way of dealing with this menace.

These, and other eighteenth-century horse brasses, were made from latten. This was sheet brass made from ingots composed of copper and calamine, flattened by means of horse- or water-operated battery hammers. Calamine is a zinc silicate which, when mixed with a little fine charcoal and heated with copper, produces globules of brass. Horse brasses made from latten bore hammer marks front and back; years of polishing may virtually have removed all traces of these marks from the front surface, but they remain visible at the back.

It must be emphasized that latten was not an alternative name for brass, but a term used to distinguish English hammered sheets from brass made by any other process. It was rarely produced after about 1830.

Brasses suspended from the martingale (Plate 1) appear to date no earlier in England than about 1830. Saddlers', brass-founders' and other pattern books have been inspected and although other harness furniture is illustrated, there is no reference to the horse brasses now collected. But by the 1860s the catalogues were showing a full complement of the brasses associated with a cart-horse harness, numbering more than 330 pieces, and fifteen to twenty of these were pendant horse brasses — a face-piece on the forehead; a pair of ear-brasses hanging behind the ears; three on each side of the runners at the shoulders; and as many as ten hanging from the martingale.

The introduction of martingale brasses appears to have been simultaneous with the discarding by military officers of the gilded copper crescent-shaped badges known as gorgets. Until 1830 officers wore these toys, either attached to the collar or suspended from the neck, hanging a little below the chin. These ornaments were direct descendants of the gorget, an important accessory in a suit of defensive steel armour covering the joint between helmet and breastplate, thus protecting the throat and the back of the neck.

As armour gradually became outmoded the gorget remained, now in gilded silver, worn with the stout buff leather coat made from buffalo skin, familiar in portraits of officers painted in the first half of the seventeenth century. Samuel Butler in *Hudibras*, 1663, wrote: 'He wore for ornament a ring and about his neck a threefold gorget.'

Eventually this gorget was reduced in size until it became a crescent-shaped toy measuring about $4\frac{1}{2}$ inches long by $3\frac{1}{2}$ inches wide. There was no back plate and the front was generally embossed with the royal arms or a crowned monogram with floral supporters. Worn throughout the reigns of Queen Anne and the four Georges, they were at first of silver parcel gilt, the arms standing out in silver against a gold background. The ends might be perforated in a fish-scale design and pierced on each horn point for insertion of the suspension chain. From the 1760s the majority were made of gilded copper, others in Sheffield plate. The coat of arms or monogram was hand-raised in eighteenth-century examples. From about 1800, following the introduction of a hard tool-steel, they were raised by means of a drop hammer.

When the wearing of military gorgets was discontinued, surplus consignments of gilded copper appear to have been acquired by chapmen who disposed of them for harness decoration at the time of the coronation of William IV in 1831. Soon gorgets were issued specially for the saddlery trade, these being made without fish-scale piercing. Finally they were made without raised ornament.

The collector, then, will find four types of toy gorgets, all of them now rare: (*a*) hand-raised in gilded silver or copper, eighteenth century; (*b*) drop-stamped in gilded silver, copper, or Sheffield plate; (*c*) drop-stamped in gilded copper without fish-scale piercings; (*d*) plain in gilded copper.

From these toy gorgets developed the trade in horse brasses which has continued uninterruptedly until the present day to enrich the dark tones of polished leather harness. The annual output of reproductions possibly exceeds the number sold in any year throughout their period of actual use. So far as manufacturing processes are concerned collectors will be able to group horse brasses into nine well-defined classes: (*a*) hand-worked from hard-textured latten or battery brass — to 1830; (*b*) hand-worked from rolled calamine brass — 1830s to 1850; (*c*) cast in fine brass alloy of the pinchbeck type — late 1830s to 1860; (*d*) cast in calamine brass — to 1860; (*e*) cast in a brass of brilliant gold colour — 1837 to 1860; (*f*) cast in zinc or spelter brass — 1860 to 1900; (*g*) stamped from rolled spelter brass — 1870s to 1900; (*h*) reproductions and souvenirs — modern; (*i*) fakes — from 1930.

The first group has already been described. Horse brasses of the second group, for sale at horse fairs and by the saddlers, were being produced by a few specialist garret masters in the Birmingham district from the mid-1830s. These were made from sheets rolled from a soft-textured, dull-looking calamine brass, invariably marred with a few surface flaws. Calamine brass, whether in the form of latten or of rolled sheets, cannot be reproduced profitably to-day.

These early brasses were chiefly sun-flashes and a crescent design with incurving horns and with a rectangular strap loop, a pair of wings extending outward from the junction of the loop and the plate.

Brass souvenirs of all kinds were issued for the coronation of Queen Victoria in 1838, including a series of cast face-pieces displaying a portrait of the queen. These were made in prince's metal, a high quality brass alloy of the pinchbeck class composed, according to George Dodd, a technical author writing in 1844, 'of about equal weights of copper and zinc.' This metal, considerably more costly than ordinary brass owing to a series of purifying processes which it underwent, could be cast in sharper relief. The chased casting was tinged to a beautiful reddish-golden hue, by heating until slightly red, then, when cold, laying it to pickle in diluted vitriol. After washing in water the brass, held in a pair of nippers, was immersed for a moment in aquafortis. The high lights were then given a final burnishing with a steel burnisher dipped in gall to prevent scratching. A second series from the same pattern was issued at the time of the queen's marriage to Prince Albert in 1840.

It has been suggested that the queen's face on these early brasses was responsible for the name face-piece as a generic term for horse brasses. But the name face-piece was applied only to those which hung on the forehead of the horse. A merchant's catalogue of the 1890s captioned such a brass as a 'cart-horse face-piece'. It has been suggested, too, and again wrongly, that they were named face-pieces because the face of the brass was polished, the reverse being merely filed.

From prince's metal, too, were made face-pieces displaying estate crests. A recognized expert in this work was Robert Hughes, 52 Clifden Street, Finsbury, London, who worked from the late 1830s to about 1865, supplying heraldic brasses to the commission of saddlers. Many of his brasses were gilded. An extensive collection of his heraldic work in gilded prince's metal and ordinary brass was shown at the Great Exhibition, 1851. Daniel Moriarty, 34 Berwick Street, Oxford, made heraldic face-pieces in cast german silver which might be either gilded or, less frequently, silver-plated. The casting patterns for these were exquisitely carved in hard mahogany and remained the property of the purchaser so that they could not be copied promiscuously.

Estate brasses might also be in the form of a cypher, with or without a coronet, within a ring or a crescent. Many of these were assembled from three castings: the frame, the coronet and the cypher, the latter being riveted into position. Later crested brasses might also be made in this way and are much less finely finished than the one-piece variety. Genuine estate brasses are comparatively rare. When examples are frequently noted bearing the same crest they must be considered to be twentieth-century souvenir brasses. Engraved crests and cyphers are sometimes to be seen on the domes of early Victorian sun-flash brasses, thus emphasizing their use as face-pieces.

Horse brasses from the opening of Queen Victoria's reign began to be made in a wider range of designs and hung upon the martingale. This was the broad band of leather, or series of straps, extending from the nose-band or reins to the girth, and by keeping the horse's head down prevented it from rearing or throwing back its head.

The shapes of horse brasses appear to have represented mainly astronomical motifs including the sun, shown as a disk with rays and often within a frame; the crescent moon which saddlers' sales talk suggested was the emblem of Diana to whom horses were sacrificed; and stars which, with eight points, were considered to have some mystic influence, and with five points were long believed to make any driven horse safe against the dangers of the road.

These emblems were quickly accompanied by one-piece brasses in which a heart or shield was framed within a drill-perforated ring with serrated edge and the polished central surface engraved perhaps with a crest, monogram or the horse's name. A hand-made crescent cut from rolled plate might contain within its horns an animal model cast in prince's metal, chased and brazed into position. Horses and lions are often found in this position.

A series of well-defined cast horse brasses made between 1837 and 1860 were of brass made from copper and spelter, by a method patented in 1781 by James Emerson. According to R. Watson, *Chemical Essays*, 1782–87, Emerson's brass was 'more malleable, more beautiful and of a colour more resembling gold than ordinary brass'. The zinc used was whiter and brighter than any other European production. This metal, smooth surfaced and brilliant gold in colour, is easily distinguished from the calamine brass which continued in use for casting until about 1860, a far less radiant metal when polished and with a surface flawed by pitting owing to the presence of air bubbles in the molten metal.

Emerson's patent, specification No. 1297 of 1781, fully describes his methods; copies of this may be had from the Patent Office, Southampton Buildings, London, E.C. 4. The spelter was melted in an iron boiler and granulated by passing through a suitably-pierced ladle into a cask of cold water. A mixture was then prepared of 54 lb. copper shot, 10 lb. finely ground calcined calamine, and about 1 bushel of ground charcoal. A handful of this was thrown into a casting pot, and upon it 3 lb. granulated spelter. The pot was then filled with the mixture. Eight other pots were made ready in the same way, this completing the charge for a nine-pot furnace. As impurities in the copper and spelter were gradually eliminated, and higher furnace temperatures made available, calamine was eventually omitted from the formula.

Emerson's patent was made possible only by the efforts of earlier investigators towards purer copper and zinc. The new process formed the basis for present-day brass founding. Considerably more than half a century elapsed before Emerson's brass came into general use during the Crimean War when brass founders were necessarily compelled to abandon obsolete methods. This copper-calamine-zinc brass had been in limited use, however, by the candlestick casters and other makers of purely decorative brassware since about 1800.

To compete with this more expensive alloy, the calamine brass founders brought into use a process by which the finished brass could be gold-tinged. Horse brasses were roughly cleansed with a weak acid solution, followed by dipping into a stronger solution. The brass was then deadened by dipping into a still stronger acid, but not so strong that its action on the metal would cause the finished work to be mottled and unsaleable. After drying in boxwood sawdust it was again dipped in acid and washed in water. High-lights in the casting might then be burnished.

For a short time in the 1850s there was a vogue for burnished

1. (*Above*) Horse brasses attached to leather martingales, loin straps and face pieces. At the top are four hame plates. 2. (*Below*) A collection of horse brasses showing a wide range of formal patterns. The bottom row also includes several bell motifs. *All in the Castle Museum, York.*

3. Horse brasses in the collection of Mr E. F. Bayden.

4. Horse brasses, showing horse shoe, corn sheaf, acorn, thistle, shamrock, and commemorative Victorian motifs. *In the Castle Museum, York.*

horse brasses to be lacquered, thus protecting the polish from the effects of damp and mud. This lacquer was prepared from spirits of wine, gum-lac, turmeric, and saffron. The horse brass was heated and the lacquer applied with a brush. This had a faintly golden hue. Colourless lacquer was not marketed until about 1920.

Leather harness after the Great Exhibition became more lavishly enriched with glowing yellow brass ornament. Formerly a golden hue had been preferred. By the early 1860s the dray and cart horses in May Day processions were wearing an ever-increasing number of brasses, enhanced with brightly coloured ribbons as streamers and plaited into mane and tail. Brasses became an every-day part of harness equipment worn by driven horses, and the martingale might display as many as ten. Lacquered brasses showed a slight dullness and carters preferred the spotless brilliance of freshly polished brass. This involved much hand-polishing which in the course of years resulted in a silky texture. No amount of mechanical polishing will produce precisely this effect.

By about 1860 the use of zinc or spelter in brass without the addition of calamine had become general. This is the brass in which the majority of horse brasses were cast. Various alloys were produced, the Walsall harness furniture trade evolving a special for-mula eminently suited to their purpose and taking on a high brilli-ance. In the early 1860s Walsall employed more than five hundred men in casting and finishing brass harness furniture, their wages being twenty shillings for a week consisting of six twelve-hour days. Birmingham was a comparable centre.

A master-pattern was carved from pear-wood. From this were prepared the actual casting patterns in prince's metal or some similar alloy, or in a tin-lead alloy; both of these produced clear-cut relief work. The actual horse brasses were cast from these in sand-moulds. Some of these alloy casting patterns have been mistaken for horse brasses and are sometimes included in collections.

The edges and interstices of the rough casting were then file-finished, piercing being carried out by drilling, and the relief designs carefully modelled with suitable tools. Finally the horse brass was smoothed and polished.

At the back of each brass when it left the mould were a pair of small projections or struts, known as 'gets'. These were produced where the molten metal entered the hollow mould. They were left intact until the brass had been polished, enabling the filer and finisher to take a grip on them in his vice. In early horse brasses the 'gets' were afterwards so carefully removed that their traces

B

are almost invisible: later, when removed by the filer, two distinct rings remained on the back of the horse brass. In a few instances the 'get' appeared on the upper edge of the strap loop and such struts have been invisibly removed by grinding. In reproductions these 'gets' remain untouched.

Machine-stamped horse brasses date from the 1870s and were made almost exclusively at Walsall and Birmingham. According to Franklin, writing in 1866, stamped brasses were already in production, but the backs of these were filled with lead. A malleable rolled brass of thin gauge was used, the finished brass weighing no more than two ounces, or less than half the weight of its contemporary cast equivalent. The metal is smooth on both sides, the relief pattern showing in reverse at the back. Low relief work needed only a single operation of the stamp, while that in high relief was carried out in three operations, the metal being annealed between each stamping to prevent it from splitting. Such horse brasses are often perforated and patterns might bear a close resemblance to earlier examples in cast brass. Surrounds are usually flat, but the inner edge may be raised to form a rim in low relief. In later stamped brasses, rims and perforations were not finished by filing as in the early productions.

The number of horse brass designs issued during the Victorian period has not been computed with any degree of accuracy. Three thousand has been suggested as a reasonable total, including the reproduction and souvenir examples of the present century. Genuine examples, issued by the harness furniture makers, would not reach half that number, however. A catalogue issued in the 1880s by an unnamed firm of merchants listed three hundred varieties, each with a pattern number. Horse brasses have been seen with these figures cast into the reverse, suggesting that this firm either owned the patterns or found it convenient to utilize the maker's pattern numbers.

In certain rare instances a horse brass will be found back-stamped with a diamond-shaped mark containing letters and numerals. This, with its central 'R^d', its four corner compartments, and its surmounting circle enclosing the Roman numeral I, show the brass to have been made between 1842 and 1883, and the design registered at the Patent Office, thus ensuring three years' protection against piracy. The various letters and figures, rightly interpreted from the key chart now at the Patent Office, tell the date on which the design was registered, and the name of the maker.

The early and mid-Victorian maker of brass harness furniture

devised horse brasses so that they had some personal association with
the purchaser's trade or district. The wagoner and his whip, for
instance, was intended mainly for Sussex farmers who long expressed
a liking for that pattern; the dolphin sold extremely well in Wilt-
shire for a reason not now known; the Staffordshire knot obviously
was at home in Staffordshire; and the wool merchant's symbol was
always stocked by saddlers in the sheep-rearing districts. At the end
of the century this aspect of horse-brass salesmanship was virtually
lost amid a spate of purely commercial productions displaying
devices in no way capable of being associated with driven horses or
trades.

Carters and others associated with agriculture could choose between a wheatsheaf (Plate 4), or a sickle inserted between the
horns of a crescent or framed within a star. Set within a crescent
might be a well-cast cart-horse and wagon or a windmill. The
wheatsheaf, known heraldically as a garb, was a highly popular
motif in the northern counties. The majority are one-piece castings
with pierced rims, but a stamped series is found in a plain crescent.
The rarest is a plain shield against which the wheatsheaf stands in
bold relief.

The agricultural series includes too what is generally described
as the shepherd with his crook; close inspection will show that this
very frequent brass is a wagoner carrying a whip, a pattern originally popular in Sussex. The shepherd is, however, known in association with a windmill. These were issued from the mid-1870s to the
late 1890s by a horse dealer who traded extensively in England
and Wales. Each horse was provided with a face-piece depicting a
shepherd and windmill. The horse dealer was William Shepherd,
Windmill Farm, Lane Head, in the Foreign of Walsall, where one
of the horse-furniture manufacturers possessed a master pattern in
wood, carved at William Shepherd's cost and from which were made
a number of casting patterns in pewter. Twelve dozen of these horse
brasses were customarily ordered at one time. William Shepherd
was long able to recognize horses that had passed through his hands
by the presence of his trade brass on their harness. Windmills were
a popular Lincolnshire motif, and one collector has more than a
dozen different patterns.

The ploughman and his horse is now a popular emblem, although
the plough alone is rarely found. Like the cow, these appear to have
been issued for present-day collectors only.

Other trades were catered for, such as a barrel for the brewer
(Plate 3). This might be used vertically in an elongated crescent to

which it was attached by four struts. The crescent was soon extended to form a circular frame into which a cast motif might be brazed. These rings might be plain or pierced, and with or without serrated edges. Alternatively the barrel remained unframed and hung horizontally as a pendant, a strap loop being brazed to one edge. A group of three tuns or barrels was common, this representing the arms of the Brewers' Company.

A large number of flamboyant birds are to be found on horse brasses, usually enclosed in a narrow cast framework, often a plain ring with a serrated outer edge, into which the bird motif, separately cast, has been inserted and brazed into position. Sometimes the bird is more carefully finished than the flat frame.

Among the birds thus to be found are the pelican and peacock. The 'pelican in her piety' depicted the bird feeding her young with blood drawn from the breast. This motif, suggestive of maternal solicitude, was sold in some districts to be hung as a face-piece on a brood mare. The peacock is found full-faced with outspread tail; walking; and side view with tail trailing on the ground. This bird was considered sacred to Hera, goddess of fertility, and such a horse brass was also considered ideal as a face-piece for a brood mare. Pelican and peacock, in the form of inexpensive pairs of brass chimney ornaments, were popular wedding gifts in the Midlands in the first half of the nineteenth century, being considered to bring good luck to a prospective mother.

Old English game-cocks, eagles and phoenixes are also found, the latter being worn exclusively by dray horses owned by the Phoenix Brewery. These date between the 1870s and the end of the century. Birds found in souvenir brasses include the swan, eagle, emu, duck, turkey, raven, ostrich, lyre bird and magpie. These, and many of the modern animals, have a family likeness in technique, suggesting a common source. The souvenir horse brass incorporating a bird or animal motif is cast in a single piece.

Among animals the horse itself was the most frequent motif (Plate 3). The prancing horse of Kent, which a thousand years earlier had decorated Saxon banners, and the horse combatant are common. Other models range from the graceful race horse to the heavy dray horse, including winged and running steeds. Those carrying an oak spray in the mouth were estate brasses of the Duke of Norfolk.

Horeshoes were, naturally enough, a common motif, being a symbol of good luck. It is surprising, however, how often they hang with the opening downward (Plate 4). They are usually cast and contain a profile portrait of a horse's head and neck looking to the left. The head is sometimes cast separately and brazed into a stamped horseshoe. In others a carthorse in relief is shown walking to the right, some finer examples being hand-finished. The cart horse is also found framed in a circle with a serrated rim. These are mostly cast, but an interesting series is stamped in relief on a plain disk of serrated outline. Horses are sometimes found in miniature form within a plain wide outer border with a serrated edge and a wide pierced inner border.

The front view of a horse's head in a quatrefoil opening, with a circular outline, is found, but the casting is usually carelessly carried out in inferior metal. Horses cast in relief and shown fully harnessed made an attractive pendant without a frame, the loop rising from the top of the horse's back. It is doubtful if these were made earlier than 1920.

A stamped or cast horseshoe with nail holes might contain a trotting horse on the slender bar joining the two horns of the shoe. Other horseshoes contain various crest-like horses, or some entirely unassociated motif. An expanded horseshoe might contain three smaller ones (Plate 4). The horse is also found within the horns of a crescent which might be pierced and the horns almost touching. In more than seventy brasses containing horse motifs in one collection there was no duplicate of the horses displayed. Race horses number about two per cent of all nineteenth-century examples in the equine series.

Sporting animals obviously had a vogue among draymen and carters. Examples were made with fox masks (Plate 3), greyhounds, hare, and stags. The bear and staff, boar, camel, lion and squirrel are lesser-known animal motifs. Souvenir animal brasses include several versions of the horse; cat, bull, cow, dog and chamois invariably belong to this group.

Acorns and thistles were widely used as motifs, both appearing first in the 1890s (Plate 4). They are found separately, the acorn often in a wide frame pierced with holes arranged in four concentric circles. Acorns and oak leaves are usually found within a crescent and cast, one series having a stamped crescent with a cast sprig brazed inside. The acorn usually points upward when alone, and downward in a sprig. The flowering thistle was a Scottish requirement and is found in many patterns. Rose, thistle and shamrock designed as a single motif are to be found, usually within a plain crescent.

Horse brasses displaying the royal crown, enclosed in a variety of frames, occasionally find their way into collections. Some of these were sold by the Office of Works at auctions of surplus goods and eventually found their way into the retail market. A number of these are stamped on the back B.P., showing them to have been in use originally at the Royal Mews, Buckingham Palace. Others were issued to the various Ministries, frames of differing design being used by each. So far no evidence has come to light by which these may be distinguished. Some of these frames were cast with inserted crowns brazed into place. Others, later, were stamped in a piece from rolled brass with the crown in relief encircled by one or two rows of piercing and a serrated edge. In some cases the date of issue was stamped into the back of the brass. These brasses must obviously be genuine collectors' pieces as, except during coronation years, it is illegal to utilize royal crests for commercial or any other purposes. The same restriction applies to the monarch's coat of arms which is found only on twentieth-century coronation horse brasses. Horses employed by the Admiralty at dockyards and elsewhere were provided with face-pieces displaying an anchor enclosed in a pierced frame, usually with serrated edges.

Horse brasses displaying portraits are, with few exceptions, of the twentieth-century souvenir variety. Ambitious depictions of royalty are obtainable, but the majority are poorly finished. The very rare 'bun' portraits of Queen Victoria in profile with a star-shaped inner rim were, no doubt, issued early in her reign. The 'widow' portraits are frequent. Those issued on the occasion of her jubilee in 1887 have an unpleasant three-quarter profile with highly perched crown and widow's weeds and might be inscribed '1837 Her Majesty's Jubilee 1887'. Less rare is the full widow profile designed by Thomas Brock and first issued on the coinage in 1893. This is found in diamond jubilee brasses (Plate 4), many being inscribed with the date, but the difference in the portrait serves to distinguish between the two jubilees. A series issued at the time of the diamond jubilee was in the form of a Victoria cross bearing a royal crown and inscribed '1837 Diamond Jubilee 1897'. Others were in the form of openwork Maltese crosses. Heart-shaped horse brasses with the front surface shaped in full relief might be inscribed 'Victoria Jubilee 1887'.

The Prince of Wales's feathers are to be found, both nineteenth-century and, more prolifically, souvenirs of the 1920s. The three feathers represent 'Good Deeds, Good Words, and Good Thoughts'. Early examples were in circular frames; later they were shaped. Usually they were cast, but a series has been noted with the three feathers stamped in a plain ring. Edward VII is found full face and in profile, both as Prince of Wales and as king. Several editions of each are known, always cast in a single piece. The frame might be inscribed 'God Save the King 1902'. Modern productions include George V, George VI, Queen Elizabeth II, the queen consorts, and the very rare Edward VIII.

Portraits of political celebrities of the late nineteenth century include Gladstone, Disraeli, Joseph Chamberlain, and Lord Randolph Churchill. These are all found in circular frames, but Disraeli might be enclosed in a border of primroses, or primroses encircled with a narrow pierced rim. Early twentieth-century issues included Shakespeare, Lincoln, John Wesley, Nelson, Wellington, Baden-Powell, Roberts, Kitchener, Lloyd George, the jockey Fred Archer, and, more recently, Sir Winston Churchill and Field-Marshal Viscount Montgomery.

The heart motif (Plate 1) is common in the stamped series, often a plain heart enclosed in a circular frame, sometimes with rayed piercing outside a ring of circular piercings. The heart appears to have been used on the check rein. Rare is the heart in a heart, a heart in relief having a heart pierced in its centre. A series of cast hearts has a secondary heart rising in relief from the centre.

Bells have always been popular for horse brasses (Plate 2), and a few originals have come to light in which the brass consists of a bell-shaped ground into which is fitted a swinging bell; in others a 'ground' with a perforated rim has a bell-shaped opening in which hangs a small bell. Examples containing three bells are known. Another type has a bracket projecting from the front of the brass, from which hangs a tinkling bell.

Sun-flashes and brasses with boss centres might have the central motif rising from a plain disk, often with a serrated edge (Plate 1). Sometimes the boss is surrounded by concentric circles in relief, their number and width varying. A splash of colour might be given from the mid-1890s by fitting into the raised centre a boss of coloured glass or bone china. Colours noted are yellow, green, dark blue, red, and ringed red, white and blue. A series of uncommon rectangular horse brasses, with incurved clipped corners, have a central small boss against a plain ground; others might be shield-shaped.

Commemorative brasses, other than the jubilee issues, appear to be of twentieth-century manufacture and all are cast. A banner-shaped horse brass was issued on the occasion of the 1919 Peace Treaty, inscribed 'Peace 1919 Victory'. The Royal Society for the Prevention of Cruelty to Animals has issued horse brasses since

1896. These are of two kinds, both inscribed 'Merit Badge'. The earlier consists of a circular disk with the royal coat of arms in the upper half and has been issued in two sizes at horse shows since that date. The other is in the form of a shield and has been issued since 1902 at the Annual Cart and Van Horse Parades in Regent's Park. Other societies also issue badges in the form of horse brasses.

Several identical devices might be united in a single horse brass such as three conjoined crescents contained within a fourth, or two crescents brazed back to back with a third below; three horseshoes within a circle of horseshoes; two bells suspended within a bell-shaped frame; a central cog-wheel surrounded by seven smaller cog-wheels; three Staffordshire knots within a ring.

Uniformity of design in brass harness furniture was customary until the 1880s. The brasses hanging from the martingale might be in matching sets of gradually diminishing sizes. These might number from four to ten, six being usual. The lowest might feature a personal symbol or a name plate. These were attached to the martingale by means of short leather straps passing through the rectangular brass loops, and copper-riveted to the martingale. The presence of machine-made bifurcated rivets suggests either a late origin, that replacements have been made, or that the strap is a modern reproduction. Original sets on the old leather martingales are rare to-day.

Locomotives are found in more than twenty patterns, the majority being issued for the various railway companies. No doubt the railway historian would recognize the types used by the various railways. They are usually displayed in crescents or pierced rings, and in some a driver is included. They were used in association with a brass bearing the monogram or initials of the company, pierced into a flat plate, covering most of the field. An old series consists of a set of six locomotives illustrating their development from the 'Rocket' until about 1880. The series is difficult to acquire complete, but collectors have been known to build up a genuine set. Another old series consists of a plain crescent engraved with a representation of the 'Rocket'. Horse brasses displaying various ships are common, but it is doubtful if any of these date earlier than 1920.

Sets of four playing-card suits, each enclosed in a flat ring pierced with pips of the same suit, formed a popular matching set, a fifth and lowest brass was sometimes included displaying an eight-pointed ring, each containing a pip in high relief. Sets of scallop shells in graduated sizes are stamped and not uncommon; single cast examples date earlier.

The lower brass on a martingale was often used by saddlers supplying sets of harness for announcing their name and address above the words 'Saddlery and Harness'. This brass was often a lunar crescent with the inscription either engraved or impressed with letter punches. Examples have been recorded in which the top brass of a martingale is cast in the form of the saddler's trade mark. At about this time martingales complete with brasses became standard harness accessories, saddlers fitting them with patterns selected at random but of a type known to find favour in the district. A fully brassed martingale recently exhibited had a Staffordshire knot at the top, then the wool merchants' symbol, a 'bun' portrait of Queen Victoria, and finally the saddlers' brass inscribed 'Ruddler Wolverhampton'.

A dated horse brass on a martingale might record the year in which the harness was bought, the date usually being found engraved upon or punched into the frame of the lowest brass. Instances have been noted, however, of special name and date brasses, plain hearts hand-cut from rolled brass and engraved with the name of the horse and a date.

A great number of the horse brasses now displayed in shops were made specially for the gift shop trade and make no pretence of reproducing authentic patterns. They are made for purposes of interior decoration, with no intention of catering for the true collector. In 1953 a small foundry was established in Kent for the express purpose of making horse brasses from original designs.

Many reproductions are sold exactly as they leave the founder's moulds apart from undergoing a process of tumbling. They are placed in a power-operated tumbler-barrel which revolves, shaking the brasses against each other and removing all traces of sand and smoothing the surface. Tumbled horse brasses are sold otherwise untouched at varying prices. In 1954 they were noted in a Staffordshire shop at two shillings and threepence each; exactly the same models, apparently from the same master-patterns, were offered in a nearby 'antiques' shop at four shillings and sixpence each. Hand-finished and processed, they were seen in London later in the same week, priced at a guinea each. These horse brasses were cast from ordinary industrial brass-founder's metal bearing only a superficial resemblance to the alloy used in Walsall.

Collectors should remember that fakes intended to deceive the serious collector abound in great numbers. Hand-made horse brasses are still being produced from rolled sheet brass, design and workmanship suggesting a common source. Some assistance in

shaping appears to come from a hand-press. The rolled metal used
is, however, of a quality easily distinguished from the early alloy
once comparison has been made with the genuine article.

Bogus brasses, however, are more usually cast and even though
workmen's time and acids have been used to give them an old
worn appearance, close inspection of inner corners of the strap loop,
which attaches the brass to the martingale or elsewhere, will
demonstrate the presence of the faker's hand which fails to simulate
exactly the effect of surfaces smoothed with years of wear by
rubbing against leather. These fakes, too, omit the rubbing and
consequent wear which occurred on the back of the lower edge of
the brass, making it appreciably thinner. When given a well-worn
appearance, however, it is difficult to distinguish a fake from a
genuine example if the alloy has been carefully chosen to match
that of Victorian prototypes. A collector searching for original
horse brasses should carry an undoubtedly genuine example for
purposes of comparison.

Horse brass collectors will naturally be interested in the wider
range of associated harness furniture. The driven horse long carried,
perched on his head, between the ears, a fly terret, known more
colloquially as a flyer or swinger. This consisted of an upright ring
in which swung a single horse brass with both faces finished and
polished. Instead of being made with a strap loop, such brasses,
which are considerably smaller in diameter than the usual horse
brass, were cast with a solid eye placed at right angles. This fitted
into a pair of lugs on the inner side of the ring-top, held in position
by a pin which enabled it to swing freely. This brass often matched
either the face-piece or the top brass on the martingale.

Not infrequently a cast and chased horse in full figure hangs
within the ring; occasionally a horse's head. A brewer might display here a miniature hooped barrel shaped in the round, either
vertical or horizontal. The martingale itself might then display a
graduated series of face-pieces ornamented with a barrel motif.

The fly terret might be mounted with a tall cylindrical brush,
often with dyed bristles, blue and red being common. In other
instances there was a tiny bell which tinkled faintly as the horse
moved.

These bells were the Victorian survivals of the latten bells which
for at least two centuries rose vertically above the collar. The bells
at first were of latten, later of hand-hammered rolled brass which
closely resembled latten. The bells were fitted in sets, one above the
other, three, four, or five, each row making its own chord. Each

set hung in its own shallow rectangular cover of brass, lined inside with leather to prevent the bells from striking the metal hood and producing discords. A set most usually consisted of four rows of bells, one upon the other, each contained in a metal hood. The lowest row, of five bells, was termed the lead; the next, of four bells, the lash; the third and fourth rows, of three bells each, were known as the body and the thill.

Hame plates (Plate 1), seldom measuring more than eight by four inches, were attached to the straps connecting the hame. The hame plate was of sheet brass, with several small versions of loop-less horse brasses riveted flat against it, sometimes within a chased border or with a cresting attached to its upper edge. Pairs of loin straps (Plate 1), one on each side of the horse's backbone, usually displayed three brasses each, and etiquette demanded that these be correctly paired.

The leather used for harness, including the martingale, in the nineteenth century was almost invariably horse hide tanned with oak bark. Horse hide combined lightness with strength and was less liable to be flawed with weevils than were cow hides. English hides were preferred, although considerably less costly supplies came from South America. An expert saddler examining a harness could tell by its texture in which district of the kingdom it had been tanned. There were special local modes of treatment, but the basic method of tanning was to steep the hide in oak bark liquor for a year, by which time the gelatine in its texture combined with the tannin from the bark and filled the pores in the hides, making them watertight.

The collector of brasses attached to a martingale will carefully inspect the leather. If it is of horse hide it may be assumed genuine; if of cow hide displaying evidence of modern chemical tanning then it, and the brasses, should be rejected. Cow hides were sometimes used for nineteenth-century harness, years of rubbing against the horse and cleaning with wax polish having made it far more pliant than modern leather. Martingales of hog skin were made in Scotland and considered by the trade to be the finest regarding wear and beauty of colour. These are rare and always genuine.

CHAPTER TWO

Silver Sugar-Tongs

HONEY-REFINING was an important luxury trade in medieval England. The earliest consignment of sugar arrived in London only late in the reign of Henry III (1216–72). This was broken into small pieces and crushed by pestle and mortar into a coarse greyish-white powder. Known as blanch-powder, a pound cost the affluent purchaser more than the equivalent of a five-pound note in present-day currency.

Until Elizabethan times all sugar came from the Indies by way of Damascus and Aleppo. Refineries were established at Venice, Genoa, Pisa, Cyprus and elsewhere in the Eastern Mediterranean, and later at Antwerp. The refining of sugar by means of washing and crystallizing in conical moulds was a Venetian invention of the late thirteenth century. This produced a much whiter sugar than formerly, but the pure white crystals familiar to-day are little more than a century old. As late as 1856 it was customary for sugar-bakers to improve the appearance of sugar loaves by coating them with white lead.

The earliest English refineries were established in London by two Venetians during 1544. Competition from the experienced sugar-boilers of Antwerp was so intense, however, that profits were negligible until after the sack of Antwerp in 1568. These refiners then reaped the reward of patience and eventually grew wealthy. London quickly became an important sugar-refining centre, and by 1660 supported about fifty sugar-bakers at a time when the total amount of raw sugar imported never exceeded 800 tons in a year. The average daily output of each refiner would approximate one hundredweight of sugar, indication that refining was a long, laborious process.

The various qualities of sugar imported into England between 1264 and 1568 were distinguished by the names of the localities in which the raw sugar was refined, such as the sugars of Venice, Alexandria, Barbary and Cyprus. Sugar-loaves were imported wrapped in corded canvas and packed in chests of a fine hardwood. Printers eagerly acquired such chests, as the wood was found ideal for block-making. Moxon, in his treatise on printing published in 1693, recorded that 'I us'd to cut blocks of Sugar-chest: That stuff being uncommonly well-seasoned, by the long lying of the Sugar in it'.

Customs officials in 1651 recognized eight classes of refined sugar at wholesale prices ranging from about threepence to three shillings a pound. These were: refined loaves, white candy, brown candy, white sugar, white sugar from British plantations, muscovadoes, penelles, and muscovadoes from British plantations. John Houghton in 1697 estimated that about sixteen million pounds of sugar were imported in 1694 for a population approximating eight million. The *Household Book* of Lady Grisell Baillie shows that during the period 1707–17 she bought only four kinds of sugar: candibord or sugar-loaf at 1s. 1½d a lb., coarse at 8d. a lb., powdered at 6d. a lb., and kitchen at 4d. a lb.

Special sugar containers for the table are not known to have been used earlier than the time of Henry VIII when a silver sugar-box and spoon accompanied the wine service. The rough wines, usually taken direct from the barrel in which they had travelled from the Continent, were sweetened and smoothed by the addition of sugar. Bacon in 1626 recorded the contemporary opinion that 'Wine Sugared inebriateth less than Wine Pure'. In 1630 members of the Pewterers' Company complained that 'Vintners buy the sugar they sell to be drunk with wine vended in taverns at 18ᵈ or 19ᵈ the pound, which they make up into 18, 19, or 20 several papers, selling each at 2d the paper, making of each pound 3/- and upwards, whereby the king is hindered in his customs, in respect that less sugar is spent with wine than would usually be if sold at a reasonable rate'. Various banqueting bills still remain in which a quantity of sugar is included with the wines, such as at a dinner given by the Goldsmiths' Company when seven gallons of canary, five gallons of claret, three gallons of white wine, and three gallons of Rhenish wine were accompanied by ten pounds of loaf sugar. This approximated to one ounce of sugar to each pint of wine.

Domestic plate inventories of the seventeenth century contain frequent references to sugar-boxes accompanied by spoons. This suggests the use of a special spoon for lifting the crushed sugar from its box. The Unton inventory of 1620 records 'a [silver] sugar boxe and one sugar boxe spoon'. An inventory made more than a century later, in 1729, refers to '1 sugar box and spoon', and '1 pair of tea tongs'.

The latter, it may be assumed, came into use during the late seventeenth century when the silver tea-equipage demanded a sugar-bowl to contain lumps of sugar royal. This was the finest

sugar then obtainable, having been trebly refined. Sugar royal added
no treacly flavour to the tea such as hostesses had customarily dis-
guised with saffron or peach leaves. Such sugar-loaves were a
favoured gift for more than a century and weighed about six
pounds. Lumps were broken from cone-shaped loaves with a sugar-
chopper and cracked into tiny pieces with the aid of polished steel
sugar-nippers somewhat resembling pliers with sharp semi-
circular blades. These small lumps were lifted from sugar-bowl to
tea-cup with the aid of sugar-tongs. The earliest reference to these
so far noted appears in W. King's cookery book published in 1708.

The earliest form of silver sugar-tongs, of which no actual
example has been noted, are seen in the silver tea-equipage shown
in the conversation-piece painted by Richard Collins *c.* 1730.
These resemble steel ember-tongs, which were made in many other
patterns, for lifting red-hot charcoal from table braziers to act as
pipe-lighters. From a U-shaped bow of springy silver extended a
pair of slender arms terminating in wide, shell-shaped grips for
picking up the sugar.

These were superseded in about 1740 by the scissor-type sugar-
tongs (Plate 6, column 1). Several goldsmiths illustrated these on
their trade-cards. Sir Ambrose Heal's collection shows patterns
made by Richard Boult 1744–53, John Fossey 1748, and John
Alderhead 1750–66. The Georgian scissor-shaped sugar-tongs
resembled a tinder-douter, with loop handles and scrolled arms
terminating in wide escallop-shell sugar-grips, their interior surfaces at first flat, then hollowed. The pivoting joint with its spring
was concealed in a flat, circular box, the plain side of which was
usually engraved with the owner's crest, monogram or initials.
The other side of the box displayed a decorative boss, usually in the
form of a rosette ornament. Much ingenuity went into designing
the scrolled and twisted arms. In some instances these were cast as
single units, in others they were built from small castings soldered
together. The finger-bows might be plain rings or shaped from
silver wire of appropriate section. Sugar-tongs of the scissor type
appear to have been in production until about 1790.

This type of sugar-tongs, like scissors themselves, included the
stork pattern popular during the third quarter of the eighteenth
century. Such tongs resembled a long-beaked stork. The body was
shaped and chased to suggest wings and feathers and the legs
ended in circular loops for the fingers. The sugar was lifted by the
beak, which opened and gripped the sugar firmly between its
serrated inner surfaces, a rivet forming the bird's eyes acting as a

pivot. A large claw was attached to one of the finger-loops enabling it to stand upon the table. In later, less carefully made, examples a cast tortoise replaced the claw.

The vogue for what were then advertised as spring tea-tongs began in about 1760. Fool-proof in action and less costly to buy, sugar-tongs of this type until about 1790 were built by soldering together three or five units: a U-shaped arch of springy silver, a pair of cast and chased arms, and two cast grips. Usually each arm and grip might be cast in a single piece. The arch was made from silver plate hammered to such a degree that the metal became springy and when bent into a U-shape automatically separated the ends of the arms after removal of pressure. These arched springs were made convex outside and concave within, the outer surface being decorated with a variety of designs in light chasing or engraving, a line border enclosing a flower or scroll ornament being favourite motifs. A space on the outer bend was reserved for the owner's crest, monogram or initials. Soldered to each end of the spring was a cast and chased arm pierced in intricate rococo designs. Some of the more open piercing was hand-cut, and so fragile were many of these sugar-tongs that breakages were frequent, repairs showing them to have occurred near to the arm-spring joint. Many pierced sugar-tong arms show casting flaws on their flat interior surfaces and file marks show clearly under a reading-glass. Grips were usually shell-shaped — occasionally in the form of acorns or leaves — with circular or oval depressions inside.

A silversmith who appears to have specialized in finely worked sugar-tongs was Thomas Wallis of London. Seven examples, all struck with the mark T.W., are illustrated in Plate 5, columns 2 and 3. A particularly fragile pair of sugar-tongs by Thomas Towman of London was given to the Victoria and Albert Museum by Queen Mary. The arms are jewelled with paste and the metal throughout is hand-wrought.

Sugar-tongs made from single strips of silver appeared during the 1780s (Plate 5, column 3, number 1). The central portion of the strip was hammered until springy, the flat tapering arms were hand-pierced, and the grips shaped with hand tools. In some instances the grips were soldered additions of cast silver. From 1790 this pattern was made with unpierced tapering arms and with spoon-shaped grips (Plate 5, columns 3 and 4). Until about 1820 arch and arms were slim, with grips plainly smooth, finely ribbed, or introducing a touch of bright-cut engraving. In some instances each grip was in the form of a tea-leaf to match an accompanying caddy

ladle. Early examples were decorated with bright-cut engraving or
simple chasing. From 1805 to 1815 ornament on sugar-tongs consisted of little more than threaded edges. Arms were then made to
match teaspoons with old English or fiddle ends. A set consisting of
half-a-dozen teaspoons and a matching pair of sugar-tongs engraved
with initials was now included as a matter of course in many an
unambitious dowry. The Bateman family of silversmiths issued
some finely designed sugar-tongs of this type.

By 1820 many sugar-tongs were made of thicker silver and the
arms were lengthened to suit the more massive sugar-bowls of the
colourful tea-sets then being made in bone china. Sugar-tongs *en
suite* with the silver sugar-bowl, however, remained slenderly
dainty, the final touch to that most lovely and well-loved collection
of English domestic silver, the tea-equipage.

The Plate Offences Act of 1739 laid down that the fee to be charged
for assaying 'every pair of tea tongs' should not exceed five farthings.
The fact that they should be included in the Act suggests that considerable numbers were being sold. The fee actually charged by the
assay office was one penny. Sugar-tongs made before 1790 were
struck only with the lion passant, national proof of sterling quality,
and with the maker's mark. These were struck, one on each arm
immediately below the arm-spring joints.

By virtue of the 1739 Act, sugar-tongs with openwork arms were
classed as 'philligree work' and consequently claimed exemption
from hall-marking. Although not required by law to be assayed,
they were voluntarily submitted to the Assay Office and struck with
the lion passant to provide purchasers with proof of sterling quality.
Statutory exemption gave makers no right to stamp anything more
than their registered maker's mark.

The Duty Act of 1784, by which sixpence an ounce was levied on
silver plate, did not affect wares exempt from marking. Sugar-tongs
are therefore not found struck with the sovereign's head duty-
mark. As date letters were not struck, collectors can decide no more
than approximately the year of manufacture. Sugar-tongs with
solid arms did not come within the schedule of exemption and consequently were struck with date letter and duty mark.

During the early nineteenth-century vogue for tea-caddies of
tortoiseshell and mother-of-pearl, spring sugar-tongs were made of
the same materials. In a series dating from 1815 to about 1835 the
tongs consisted of an arch of springy silver linked by rivets to arms
of mother-of-pearl carved with shell-shaped grips and surface
decoration. Others possessed ivory arms, similarly carved, and fitted

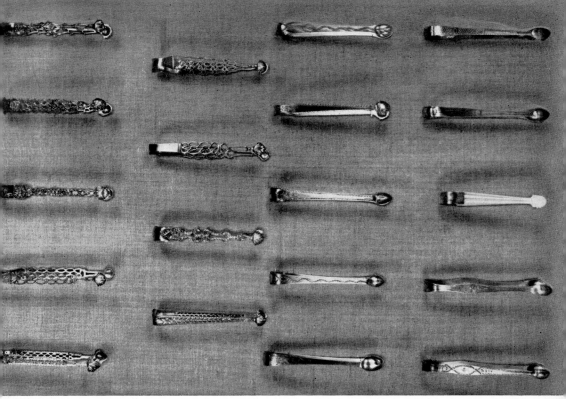

5 and 6. Silver sugar-tongs. (*Above*) The centre pair in the left-hand column, made by Thomas Towman, belonged to Queen Mary. The remainder are spring tongs dating to about 1810. (*Below*) Those on the left are of the mid-eighteenth-century scissor type; the remainder are spring tongs, pre-1790. *Victoria and Albert Museum.*

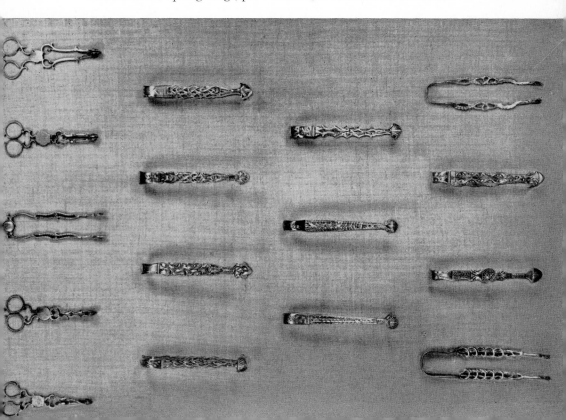

7. (*Above*) Three snuff-rasps of carved wood. The lids swivel on a joint at the wide end to expose the perforated grater fixed over a shallow recess. The snuff was removed through a grooved channel cut in the narrow end. 8. (*Below*) A table snuff-mull made from a large ram's horn. *Victoria and Albert Museum.*

to the spring arch by means of deep thin slots cut into their ends and each held firmly by three silver rivets. Alternatively, the arches might be of tortoiseshell. Birmingham was the chief place of manufacture, but such sugar-tongs were also made at Sheffield and Clerkenwell.

CHAPTER THREE

Snuff-Boxes, Mulls and Rasps

THE elegant Englishman of the Tudor or Stuart period would seldom stir from his home without his pomander or perforated pouncet box. From these he inhaled aromatic perfumes in a day when sanitation was extremely primitive. When, late in the sixteenth century, finely pulverised tobacco leaf was introduced to this country, it was carried in a pounced box and quickly established itself as a pungent protection against ill odours.

Although authorities usually assume that snuff was unknown in England until late in the seventeenth century, Dekker, in his *Gull's Hornbook*, 1609, says that 'the gallant must draw out his tobacco-box, then ladle the cold snuff into the nostril . . .'. Snuff-taking was, however, infrequent in England until the late 1670s, the English preferring to smoke rather than to inhale their tobacco. James Norcock of the Strand, who advertised in 1683, is the first so far noted as a 'Snuffmaker selling all sorts of Snuffs, Spanish and Italian'.

Snuff-taking was already well-established in Scotland, however. The Scots who accompanied the court of James I introduced to London the 'sneeshing miln', now known to collectors as the Scottish mull. For more than three centuries snuff-mulls were carried by most Scotsmen.

The 'sneeshing miln', the earliest distinctive container for snuff, was made of a ram's horn, the exterior highly polished, the interior cut with closely-spaced sharp ridges from the top to near the bottom. This ridging enabled the user to grind his own snuff from a plug of tobacco. The small end of the horn was artificially curled into a scroll, and the large end fitted with a hinged cap which might be of embossed or plain silver, or of ivory, horn or bone, fitted into a metal mount. The centre of the cover might be enriched with a cut cairngorm, agate or other semi-precious stone excavated from the Scottish mountains. At the front of the horn a small silver shield might be fixed, engraved with the owner's crest or monogram. Attached to the mull by a fine chain might be a snuff-spoon, and a hare's foot for dusting snuff from the upper lip. By the early eighteenth century serrations within the horn were no longer required by those who preferred ready-made snuff.

The *Household Book* of Lady Grisell Baillie records that in 1707 she paid four pounds 'for 3 snuf milnes'. That differentiation was made between snuff-mull and snuff-box is shown by Smollett's comment in 1771: 'The lieutenant pulled out, instead of his own Scotch mull, a very fine gold snuff-box.'

Snuff-mulls about eight inches high, designed for communal use on the table, were fashionable from early in the eighteenth century until about 1850 (Plate 8). Such a mull was made from a large ram's horn with a spiral of one-and-a-half turns. The small end was cased with plain silver, the large end fitted with a silver box to contain the snuff. The horn stood on ball feet of silver, permitting the mull to be pushed smoothly over the table-top. Attached by chains might be a mallet, pricker, rake, spoon and hare's foot.

When snuffing became a recognized custom in England during the last quarter of the seventeenth century, snuff-takers carried their own tobacco rasps. A plug of tightly rolled tobacco was drawn a few times over the small, sharp-toothed rasp. The rough powder so produced was placed upon the back of the hand and snuffed up the nose. The snuff-taker of the seventeenth and early eighteenth centuries usually carried a cylindrical box of silver or brass about two inches long. This was centrally divided, hinged covers at the ends enclosing a small iron rasp and a plug of tobacco. From about 1700 the rasp might be replaced by a perforated grater. This might be fitted into the length of the cylinder, the metal cut away being converted into a hinged protecting cover. The plug of tobacco was carried within the cylinder. The pocket snuff-grater formed from the shell of the tropical stag cowry, mounted with a silver grater, acting also as a lid, was popular during the eighteenth century. The numerous patterns made in silver may be dated by their hallmarks.

The fashionable snuff-taker from about 1690 might carry an elaborately carved case for his snuff-grater. This might be of wood or ivory, two to three inches in length. Boxwood, pearwood and walnut were usual, and might be inlaid with ivory and coloured woods, or decorated with highly coloured japan. Dean Swift has recorded that in 1711 he prepared his snuff from a fine snuff rasp-case of ivory. These rasp-cases were flat and tapering, the carved lid swivelling on a joint at the wide end. When the lid was swung open a perforated grater was revealed, fixed over a shallow recess in the lower section. The snuff was removed through a grooved channel cut in the narrow end.

For use with these snuff-rasps and graters tobacco leaves were pressed or curled into plugs or *carottes*. The term *carotte* dates from early in the seventeenth century when tobacco was prepared in the form of a carrot to be ground in a mull, later to be rasped and inhaled. Tobacco thus freshly ground into snuff was known as *tabac rapé*. From this rappee, a coarse snuff made from the darker and ranker tobacco leaves, derived its name.

Pharmacist dispensers of snuff prepared and blended special snuffs for private customers, using a giant rasp over a foot long. As the black-boy was the tobacconist's trade sign, so the rasp became the symbol distinguishing the snuff-maker's shop. The average snuff-taker, however, bought factory milled and blended snuff, and special brands were quickly on the market. In 1760 Doctor Johnson was still rasping his own snuff because ready-made rappee was liable to be adulterated with chicory leaves steeped in tar oil.

Beau Nash introduced to London society the luxurious jewelled snuff-box such as had sparkled for more than thirty years at the court of France, thus raising snuffing to the status of an elegant grace. By 1705 the handling of the snuff-box and the correct way of conveying the dust to the nostrils had become an important social accomplishment. Schools were established for teaching the art of snuff-taking. An advertisement in No. 138 of *The Spectator* 1711 outlined the curriculum of such a school:

'The exercise of the snuff-box according to the most fashionable airs and motions, in opposition to the exercise of the fan, will be taught with the best plain or perfumed snuff, at Charles Lillie's, perfumer, in the Strand, and attendance given for the benefit of young merchants about the Exchange, for two hours every day at noon, at a toy shop near Garraway's coffee-house. There will be taught the ceremony of the snuff-box, rules for offering snuff to a stranger, a friend, or a mistress, with an explanation of the careless, the scornful, the politic, and the surly pinch, and the gestures proper to each of them'.

The fashionable snuff-taker carried his box in the left-hand pocket. When it was withdrawn the snuff-taker gave the cover three smart taps near to the hinge. The box was then opened and a pinch of snuff placed on the back of the left hand or on the thumb nail, and inhaled. More frequently, however, the pinch of snuff went directly to the nose. Sneezing, of course, formed no part of ceremonial snuff-taking. The snuff-box was tapped to attract the powder away from the mouth of the box so that the opening of the lid produced no unexpected cloud of dust; three taps were considered lucky.

9. (*Above, left*) 18 carat gold snuff-box with engine-turned basket pattern on lid, sides and rising base; cover and base bearing applied mounts in yellow-gold leaf design. Date 1811. (*Above, right*) Snuff-box in 18 carat gold: lid set with rural dancing scene.

10. (*Right*) Table snuff-box in chiselled gold scroll and floral work by A. J. Strachan. Miniature, of a member of the Ward family, by Andrew Plimer. Date 1808.

11. (*Below, left*) Gold snuff-box with hunting scene engraved on lid. By D. Sutherland, about 1810.

12. (*Below, right*) Silver-gilt table snuff-box, the lid showing a still-life subject modelled and chased in high relief. London, 1819. *All by courtesy of Messrs Asprey & Co. Ltd.*

The Plot first hatcht at Rome
by the Pope and Cardinals

The Conspirators Signing ye Resolue
for killing the King

Father Conyers Preaching against ye
Oathes of Aligance & Supremacy

Dr Oates discouereth ye Plot to
ye king and Councell

Ct bedlow discouerer
of the plott

Cap bedlow examined by ye secret
Comitte of the house of
Commons

Pickerin attempts to kill ye K.
in St James Park

Pickerin Executed

St William waller burning Popish
books Images and Reliques

13 and 14. (*Above*) Lambeth wall tiles painted in blue with incidents of the Titus Oates plot of 1678, copied from a pack of engraved playing cards, about 1680. (*Below*) Liverpool printed tiles with rococo borders: (*left*) skating scene; (*centre*) battledore and shuttlecock; (*right*) the Boar and the Hound from Aesop's *Fables*.

In 1788, when snuff-taking was at its height, the *Ladies Journal* calculated that the habitual snuff-taker took a pinch every ten minutes, and this, with the ceremony of blowing and wiping the nose occupied one and a half minutes. In a snuff-taking life of forty years two years would be dedicated to 'tickling the nose', and two more years to blowing it.

The snuff-taker had a wide selection of ready-made snuffs from which to choose: sweet, strong, and salt; plain, fine, and coarse; dry, semi-moist, and moist; scented with rose, lemon, verbena, bergamot, and cloves. Many snuffers perfumed inexpensive snuffs by carrying a tonka bean in the snuff-box. Sold as 'snuff beans', these were black, almond-shaped seeds from the *dipterix odurata* tree of Guiana.

The most popular of the finer snuffs made during the eighteenth century was known as maroco, made from the following formula: 'Take forty parts of French or St Omar tobacco with twenty parts of fermented Virginia stalks in powder; the whole to be ground and sifted. To this powder add $2\frac{1}{2}$ pounds of rose leaves in fine powder. The whole must then be moistened with salt and water and thoroughly incorporated. After that it must be worked up with salts of tartar, and packed in lead to preserve its delicate aroma.'

Gentlemen laid down snuff as they laid down cellars of wine. Lord Petersham left £3,000 worth of snuff in his cabinets when he died. For the fastidious the snuff used in the morning was not suitable for the evening. There were morning, afternoon and evening snuffs and for each its appropriate box.

Women snuff-takers of the eighteenth century usually took their snuff by means of a tiny spoon or nose shovel, a custom responsible for the complaint:

> *To such a height with some is fashion grown*
> *They feed their very nostrils with a spoon.*

This device kept the nails clean and had the advantage of excluding other people's fingers from one's powder. The snuff spoon was usually of silver, about two inches long, with a shallow oval bowl; others were shaped like shovels or ladles. They are seldom found with hall-marks, as few weighed more than five pennyweights. Snuff-spoons were usually included among the fitments of the eighteenth-century étui.

For more than a century the snuff-box occupied the position in national life held by the cigarette case to-day and appeared in a wide variety of materials, from jewelled gold and solid crystal to brass and pewter. When snuff-taking was first introduced into the fashionable drawing-room, the finest goldsmiths, jewellers and enamellers were employed to create boxes resplendent with precious stones. Each rivalled the other in creating works of art that would demonstrate the exquisite taste of their owner. At this time bonbonnières of precious metals inlaid with flashing jewels were devised as gifts for women. These contained breath-sweetening comfits, and it is difficult to distinguish them to-day from snuff-boxes. By the middle of the eighteenth century such boxes might be used to contain sponges soaked in aromatic vinegar. Sir Ambrose Heal's collection of trade cards includes several illustrating such 'spunge boxes'.

Jewelled boxes of the Queen Anne period mostly had rounded corners; the oval shape tended to outnumber circular boxes during the reigns of the first two Georges, and from about 1760 until the end of the century the rectangular snuff-box found favour. Although these were the prevailing shapes in the eighteenth century, no real classification is possible, however, for every geometrical shape was taken into use. Goldsmiths worked with freedom, not only in form, but in material, colour and decoration. Comparatively few are found with hall-marks earlier than 1750.

Great pride was taken in the possession of a wide variety of gold and jewelled snuff-boxes as an indication of personal wealth and standing. Celebrities displayed magnificent collections, mostly received as gifts. During the reign of George III it became customary for the winter snuff-box to be heavy; that for the summer light. Table snuff-boxes (Plate 10) were passed with the wine after dinner and a mantel-box was an accessory found in every well-furnished room. In a debate in the House of Commons on the Civil List in 1823 it was noted that expenditure on snuff-boxes was £7,000 a year. Complaint was also made that snuff-boxes to the value of almost £15,000 were given to secretaries of state and foreign ministers on the signing of any treaty. George IV collected several hundred magnificent gold and jewelled snuff-boxes, most of which Queen Victoria had converted into personal jewellery.

A long series of splendid snuff-boxes was constructed of gold in various hues, sometimes as many as four different alloys being used in a single box. Goldsmiths produced some extremely fine effects by using red, blue and green golds against a yellow background, motifs in the design being emphasized by burnishing. The addition of silver to gold produces a green alloy. Copper will make a reddish gold, iron a bluish tint.

Another magnificent eighteenth-century series of gold snuff-boxes had lid and sides elaborately chased. In these the goldsmith worked the metal inward from the outer surface. In repoussé work the gold is worked from the back of the design. Ciselé-work is a process of carving into the surface of the metal as though it were wood. One, two or three of these processes, with the addition of engraving, may be found in a single snuff-box.

Goldsmiths, with the assistance of artist enamellers, produced some spectacular snuff-boxes. The enamelled picture in brilliant colours might be painted directly to the lid and sides of the box, a method now termed *en plein* by collectors. Others, less expensively, were set with gold plaques displaying colourful pictures commissioned from artist enamellers. *Bassetaille* enamelling, seldom found on English snuff-boxes, consists of cutting designs into the surface of the gold and applying enamel through which the translucent pattern in gold lines is visible.

Miniature portraits on ivory enrich the lids of many snuff-boxes (Plate 10). The fine grain of the ivory displays the brilliance of the painted colours, which harmonize perfectly with their surrounding gold. The majority of portraits have a personal interest only, the sitters now for the most part being unknown. A picture of a celebrity is usually indication that the snuff-box was originally a present from the person portrayed. The *tabatière à secret* has a miniature portrait concealed beneath the central motif of the cover which can only be opened by pressing a secret spring. Others have erotic paintings concealed in this space. In some combinations of snuff- and patch-box, a compartment for patches is set beneath the central motif of the cover.

Throughout the period exquisite snuff-boxes were cut in the solid from semi-precious stones such as jade and crystal. These were fitted with exquisitely wrought gold mounts. Gold mounts and hinges for jewelled snuff-boxes were always made with watch-maker's precision; the existence of the slightest defect should arouse suspicion as to the genuineness of the snuff-box.

Silver snuff-boxes were made in vast numbers, some constructed from plate and others cast, some overburdened with ornament and others smoothly plain. A comprehensive collection would include specimens bearing hall-marks from the 1690s to the 1850s. Among the late Georgian and early Victorian variants are those ornamented with niello work. The boxes were incised with ornamental patterns and the lines filled with a black metallic substance produced by melting together silver, copper, lead and sulphur. After being reduced to a powder, this was applied to the incised lines fusing into

them when heated in a muffle. The niello was then ground down
to the surface of the silver and polished.

Colourful effects were produced in the nineteenth century by
fashioning the snuff-box in agate or other variegated hard stone to
which chased silver or silver gilt was harnessed. The silver was cut
into the form of birds, flowers and foliage with scrollwork and cartouches and applied to top and sides of the box, the piercings so
arranged that the stone became a background to the silver motifs.
Such harnessing might be enriched with tiny diamonds or colourful
gemstones.

Damascening was another form of ornament found on silver and
steel snuff-boxes. Incised designs cut into the metal were filled with
wires of gold. The lines were cut in such a way that the gold was
firmly held when beaten into them.

Snuff-boxes were among the first objects to be made in that rival
of sterling silver, Sheffield plate, the pull-off covers hand-embossed
in low relief. They were circular or oval and might be fitted with
tortoiseshell linings, for until the early 1770s Sheffield plate was
silvered only on one side. After the introduction of double-plated
metal hinged snuff-boxes were made, smooth or ornamented with
bright-cut engraving. These proved to be formidable competitors
of cheap silver snuff-boxes.

Tortoiseshell snuff-boxes were made from about 1750, fashion
demanding light-coloured shell during the eighteenth century,
dark from about 1820. The shell is formed in very thin layers about
three times as long as they are wide. These layers are easily
softened by heat and can be welded together into any shape or
thickness. Its fine texture and translucent hues, and the fact that it
seldom cracks or warps, make tortoiseshell an ideal setting for gold-
point inlays. Light work in this medium is known to collectors as
piqué d'or, heavy work as *clouté d'or*. A fine *clouté d'or* series of
circular snuff-boxes has lids carved with landscapes and human
figures in deep relief. Miniatures are also found set in the lids of
tortoiseshell snuff-boxes.

The habit of snuff-taking spread to more plebian folk from about
1760. This led to a great demand for inexpensive snuff-boxes in
which durability was a first essential, since constant opening and
shutting quickly wore the lid, causing it to fit badly and spill snuff
into the pocket. The majority of these boxes were of turned boxwood and were plain, round and undecorated. These are now of
small intrinsic value.

One series of circular wooden snuff-boxes attractive to the

collector have their lids carved with the heads of saints, royal personages and other celebrities. From early in the nineteenth century such boxes might have screw-on covers.

Circular boxes made from thunga wood are also collected. In these the lid was turned to fit tightly over the collar of the box. The lid was processed and a pattern in deep relief pressed into its surface. Designs included records of topical events, portraits, scenic views, and classical groups. Some of the finer of these boxes were lined with a veneer of highly polished tortoiseshell. Plain boxes were made of petrified wood, olive-wood, rosewood, ebony, sandalwood, amboyna and palms cut across the grain.

In the nineteenth century hard-woods were skilfully carved into a wide variety of shapes such as shoes, hats, faces, animal heads, watches, bellows, fans, pistols. There was also a vogue for wooden snuff-boxes made from historical relics. The deck planks of the *Victory*, the table on which Wellington wrote his Waterloo despatch, Shakespeare's mulberry tree, Sarah Siddons's desk, Crabbe's cudgel, were all turned into snuff-boxes. Bogus relics were made, for the number turned from Crabbe's cudgel would have made a gross of this useful weapon. The number of wooden snuff-boxes reputed to have been carried by John Bunyan, Oliver Cromwell and Prince Charles Edward has reached alarming proportions, many a specimen containing a fragment of yellowed hand-made paper that bears an inscription in faded ink purporting to authenticate its origin.

Tartan-decorated snuff-boxes were made in Scotland from about 1825 until the early 1860s. The industry was founded at Laurence-kirk by James Sandy, who carved the boxes, painted them with tartans, and fixed gold or silver name-plates. By 1831 the craft had reached considerable proportions, almost one hundred people being employed in their manufacture at Old Cumnock alone. The bodies of these snuff-boxes were cut from solid sycamore wood.

One rare type of Scottish snuff-box has five lids and containers: top, bottom, ends and one side. The wood hinges and joints are near-invisible, the box appearing to be a solid block of sycamore or applewood measuring four and three-quarter inches by two and three-quarter inches.

Pewter snuff-boxes were made of metal having a high lead content, and mostly date from about 1800. Many were cast in shapes resembling miniature shoes, animal heads and so on, enriched with brightly coloured paints and gilding. Others were poorly finished replicas of the oblong and oval boxes made in silver, hinges being of the five-lug type. Rarely is an example found struck with the pewterer's mark, as heavily leaded pewter did not comply with the high standards demanded by the Pewterers' Company. Some are being made to-day of high-quality pewter and struck with bogus marks to suggest the early eighteenth-century period.

Papier-mâché boxes were found to keep snuff cool and moist more satisfactorily than any container except lead. Vast quantities appear to have been pressed from a synthesis of paper pulp, gum arabic or lacquer, and china clay. This was moulded into the desired shape, varnished, finished with rotten stone, japanned, and finally coated with varnish. Small rectangular pocket boxes, plain black or marbled, were in the majority. The lids of some early examples from about 1770 were decorated with miniatures of well-known paintings in oils. In the nineteenth century a wide range of picture lids was painted.

Fashionable snuff-boxes for the table from about 1810 were of papier-mâché with colourful paintings in oils decorating their lids. These were light, durable boxes which never cracked or warped, the soft, black japanned surface forming an excellent ground for the painter's brush. These flat-lidded boxes are circular, measuring from four to eight inches in diameter and from half an inch to one and a half inches in depth. The early lid had no encircling rim, the painting covering the entire surface. From about 1830 the cover rim was made slightly higher than the flat surface, forming a black surround to the picture. All-over paintings are usually of finer workmanship than those of the later period; the boxes also are more strongly constructed.

The manufacture and decoration of table and mantel snuff-boxes was a special branch of the papier-mâché trade. By far the greater number of covers were skilfully painted with miniature copies of well-known paintings taken from engravings. The head-artist might paint a commercially practicable version which assistants and pupils copied leaving him to add the finishing touches. In the early group of boxes, however, the collector will sometimes find an original painting not taken from an engraving: these are the most valued.

An early master-decorator of such snuff-boxes was Samuel Raven of Birmingham, whose work is assiduously collected. It is believed that he learned the art of painting on papier-mâché at the firm of Small and Son, Guest, Chopping and Bill, severing his connection when the firm was acquired by Jennens and Bettridge in 1816. This firm supplied the early, finely finished black boxes which he decorated with notable skill. After about 1830, in the face of competition from Wolverhampton, he decorated boxes of poorer quality supplied by another firm. Like many industrial artists in Birmingham, Raven appears to have been able to adapt paintings in a wide range of styles to suit the limitations of size and shape imposed by the snuff-box design.

Snuff-boxes painted by Raven and issued from his studios after about 1826 are inscribed in red script within the cover 'S. Raven Pinxt. Patronised by H.R.H. the Duke of Sussex and Prince Leopold of Saxe-Coburg', sometimes omitting the words 'of Saxe-Coburg'. Occasionally the title of the picture appears also, usually in cream paint. When the painting on the lid is entirely the work of Raven it is signed, often in script so small as scarcely to be visible without a magnifying glass. Samuel Raven always added finishing touches to paintings by his pupils.

An apprentice employed by Samuel Raven from 1820 to 1827 has recorded that his master specialized in painting pictures on box-lids and the sides of cigar-cases. During those years every picture painted in Raven's studios was copied from an engraving; no original work being produced. At this period Wilkie's early works, unprotected by copyright, were popular subjects, and snuff-box lids might be decorated with 'The Blind Fiddler', 'Rent Day', 'Blind Man's Buff', 'The Cut Finger', or 'The Village Politicians'. Burnet's painting, 'Young Bird', and 'The Beeswing' by Kidd were other favourites. 'The Proposal' and 'Congratulations' after the paintings by G. H. Harlow and engraved by H. Meyer were repeated times out of number by his pupils, each of whom reproduced the work in colours of his own choosing.

By 1830, however, the demand for these painted table-boxes had spread to a wide and less monied public. German imports satisfied their less discriminating needs, and to meet the competition English manufacturers responded with boxes of cheaper construction than formerly and less carefully painted.

Table and mantel snuff-boxes were made by at least three firms in Wolverhampton employing artists who were expert in miniature copying. Unfortunately none of these is known to have been signed. The subject of the painted decoration might be religious, royal, sporting, feminine or theatrical. Depictions of Venus were greatly favoured during the 1840s and many were issued after Titian's painting in the Uffizi Gallery, Florence. A copyist expert in reproducing Etty's works in miniature was employed by Edward Perry, Paul Street, Wolverhampton, and the many lids showing 'Venus with Doves' from R. Westall's painting came from the same source.

Snuff-boxes of similar shape and size were made of pressed papier-mâché from about 1845, many being decorated with transferred engravings. The picture was printed in oil or varnish ink upon a special transfer tissue paper. This was steeped for a few minutes in a solution consisting of one ounce of hyposulphite of soda to one quart of water. The papier-mâché lid was prepared by being japanned in a creamy tone, then coated with a varnish composed of two ounces of Venetian turpentine, one ounce of gum sandarac, one drachm of mastic, and eight ounces of spirits of wine. The transfer was laid face downward upon it, and well pressed by hand. The flimsy paper was then carefully rubbed away with oil of turpentine. This left the line-engraving showing clearly on the light surface of the papier-mâché lid. In some instances the engraving was coloured and gilded.

To protect the picture it was coated with varnish prepared from a solution of two ounces of sandarac, two drachms of mastic, and one ounce three drachms of spirits of wine. In better-quality examples a fine polish was secured by rubbing with a ball of woollen cloth dipped in mastic varnish. Later it became customary to paste an engraved paper disk to the lid. In Scotland table snuff-boxes of black wood were decorated in imitation of papier-mâché.

Snuff-boxes were made in every conceivable material: ivory, amber, porcelain, painted enamels, carved mother-of-pearl — all were made into boxes of high artistic excellence. Horn boxes lined with tortoiseshell and fitted with silver mounts had lids carved with hunting or tavern scenes, figures and animals being in light relief against backgrounds stained dark brown. Pinchbeck, japanned iron, Tunbridge ware, and bone decorated with a hot needle are all numbered among the materials of collectable snuff-boxes.

15 and 16. Transfer-printed tiles by Sadler and Green, Liverpool. (*Above*) In black, illustrating Aesop's *Fables*: the Crow and the Pitcher; the Stag and the Lion; the Wolf and the Sow; and the Stag Drinking. (*Below*) Two tiles from the celebrated theatrical set: the print of Miss Younge illustrates Bell's *British Theatre*, 1776–1777. *All in the Victoria and Albert Museum*.

17. Every detail, apart from the faces, of this mid-seventeenth-century wire-framed beadwork tray is as bright and vivid as when Sarah Gurnall dated it August 24th, 1659.

18. Two fine beadwork bags, that at the top dating to the late eighteenth century, decorated with a graceful monogram, and that below in the nineteenth-century manner, meticulously neat and full of rich colour, bead fringed and fitted with mount and chain of steel. To the sides are nineteenth-century beadwork purses. *All in the Victoria and Albert Museum.*

CHAPTER FOUR

Decorative Tiles

THE gleaming oriental porcelain imported into Europe by the Dutch East India Company during the late sixteenth century was unshipped at Amsterdam. The finest of this porcelain was so greatly admired that connoisseurs or their agents were waiting on the quay-side when fresh cargoes were due from the Indies. Enviously the Dutch potters set to work to evolve a competing porcelain. This resulted in the creation not of porcelain but of the now celebrated delft ware which they decorated either in the newly discovered cobalt blue, or in polychrome, or in black enriched with Chinese motifs in yellow and green to suggest lacquer. For long the Dutch styled their new earthenware as porcelain: importers of Chinese porcelain then distinguished their superbly beautiful ware as 'true porcelain'.

Delft ware, originally made in a group of potteries established around the Dutch town of Delft, is a blended earthenware coated with tin-enamel, decorated and then glazed. The name delft became a generic term for tin-enamelled earthenware which was really a development of maiolica adapted to imitate oriental products. The first maiolica to be made in England was at Norwich where two Flemish potters set up a kiln in 1567 to make 'gally paving tiles and vessels for apothecaries and others'. One of them, Jacob Janson, with four Flemish colleagues, is recorded as working in Aldgate London, in 1571.

In the Birmingham museum are various wall tiles taken from Gorhambury, Lord Verulam's home near St Albans, built at this time by the Bacon family, whose crest they bear. These, painted in blue, green and orange, are possibly examples of the 'gally paving tiles' made by Janson. The word 'paving' was soon dropped for in 1626 Bacon referred to them as galley-tiles, as did Delft in 1719. The Oxford Dictionary defines galley-tile as 'a glazed tile used for wall decoration'.

By the end of the century other maiolica potters were established at Lambeth and during the next hundred years the trade flourished also in Clerkenwell, Bermondsey and Deptford. English maiolica was not in any way comparable with the Dutch delft ware imported in a wide variety of articles including wall tiles. These might be white or patterned, the latter usually being ornamented with designs in cobalt blue.

English delft ware was not made until 1671 when John Ariens van Hamme was granted a patent for 'makinge tiles and porcelane and other earthen wares after the way practised in Holland'. It is significant that tiles are mentioned first, suggesting that Van Hamme was fully aware of a wide potential demand. Unfortunately a detailed account of the processes involved was not incorporated with the published specification. The granting of this fourteen-year monopoly was followed a few months later by a proclamation of Charles II 'prohibiting the importation of any kind or sort of painted earthenware whatsoever'. Van Hamme appears to have licensed his patent to others for several delft ware potters were operating in Lambeth by 1676. Soon the trade extended to Bristol, Liverpool, Wincanton in Somerset, Wednesbury in Staffordshire, and elsewhere.

In Holland delft ware tiles might cover an entire wall of a living-room, the patterned tiles being arranged in well-composed effects. The immaculate Dutch used them lavishly in kitchens, pantries, dairies, passages in domestic quarters, and in many other ways about the house. Similar uses were found for them in England where they were also greatly used in cellars and vaults. Coffee- and punch-houses and other places of public resort for the well-to-do made great use of the sanitary and light-reflection value of such tiles. Mortimer's *Husbandry*, 1707, suggests that fireplaces set with delft ware tiles were newly fashionable, facings being set with single, double, or triple rows. Throughout their period of manufacture English-made hand-painted delft ware tiles were usually referred to as Dutch or Flemish in recognition of the original source of supply. Chambers's *Cyclopaedia*, 1727, recorded that 'Flemish tyles are commonly used plastered up in the jaumbs of chimney-corners'.

Fine earthenware clays were exported from England to Holland where the tile-wright blended them with two or three native clays. The Dundry clay of Bristol was highly appreciated by the Dutch and other west country pockets were also exploited. The Dutch blending clays contained calcium carbonate and collectors can distinguish between Dutch and English tiles by testing the clay with dilute hydrochloric acid. On Dutch tiles the acid effervesces because calcium carbonate is present; there is no reaction on English tiles.

Dutch processes of tile-making differed from those used by

English delft ware potters in that decoration was applied to the biscuit; in England it was painted over the vitrified enamel. Suitable clays were washed and, in the better quality tiles, blended, while sand might be added. English potters of the eighteenth century appear to have used kilns capable of a higher temperature than those of the Dutch for the resulting ware is more vitreous and denser of texture: the Dutch is comparatively soft and porous and can be cut with a knife.

After shaping, the tiles were fired to a biscuit in a kiln emitting an equable temperature, thus preventing shrinkage and reducing the wastage caused by warping. Uniformity of size and flatness of surface without flaws or firecracks were essential tile requirements, more difficult to achieve before about 1740 than afterwards. The groups illustrated demonstrate the difficulty of controlling shrinkage in the oven. Individual tiles in the Titus Oates set (Plate 13) show slight variations in size. Examination of examples from which the enamel has partially flaked suggests that the biscuit surface might on occasion be trimmed by holding flat against a horizontal revolving stone or rubbing on a flat stone.

The biscuit tiles were vigorously brushed to remove dust and then dipped into white tin oxide enamel held in suspension by water. Hugh Owen suggests this to have been composed of 50 parts tin oxide, 65 parts frit, half a part smalt, and 5/100 part of red copper filings. The frit was prepared by fusing together 50 parts sand, 6 parts salt, and 3 parts soda. The whole was ground to an impalpable powder with water. This formula closely resembles one published by Blancourt in 1699. In the case of Dutch tiles, after dipping the moisture was absorbed into the porous biscuit, carrying with it fine particles of enamel deeply into its texture and also leaving the surface covered with a layer of fine white powder. They were then placed aside to air-dry.

The Dutch potters painted directly over this surface, afterwards sprinkling it with a thin coating of powdered lead glaze. The ware was then fired a second time, the heat converting the powder into an opaque film of white enamel, thicker and smoother than was usual on English tiles. This concealed the tint of the body. The combination of enamel, glaze and colour produced a brilliance almost equal to that of the over-glaze enamels on porcelains.

The English tile-makers enamelled over the biscuit but then gave a second firing before painting and glazing. The denser and more vitreous texture of the tile prevented the enamel from penetrating as in Dutch tiles; consequently the surface was less even.

The addition of smalt to the enamel assisted in concealing the tinge of the tile itself which might otherwise be faintly visible.

The enamelled tiles were now ready for hand-painting, usually in cobalt, occasionally with the addition of over-glaze colours. As tiles were seldom costly productions, designs were mostly carried out on small-scale mass-production lines. The pattern was outlined on the tin-enamelled tile by pouncing fine charcoal powder through a pinpricked paper stencil, the artist completing the design with speedy freehand work. Zaffre, a preparation of cobalt oxide, was ground with oil of spike lavender on a marble slab and applied with pencil brushes made by the decorators themselves from ox bristles. Shading effects were accomplished with various qualities of the same pigment. The flat tints of zaffre sometimes appear as though the colour had curdled during firing. Such a defect suggests a tile to be of English origin. Fine work was carried out with the more costly cobalt product known as smalt and some exceptional work has been noted to be in ultramarine. The less popular violet or puce decoration was obtained by using manganese oxide as a pigment. After air-drying the tiles were lightly coated with lead glaze sprinkled from a short stiff hair-brush and then fired. The heat caused the glaze to spread over the enamel like a smooth clear varnish, and in fact it was so termed by the delft ware potters. The backs of many English tiles were coated with clear lead glaze.

The Lambeth makers of delft ware tiles, although perhaps not a numerous group, appear to have employed a number of outstanding decorators. The Van Hamme establishment no doubt introduced highly experienced painters in cobalt blue from Holland, and such a one was no doubt responsible for the set of nine Titus Oates tiles now in the Schreiber Collection at the Victoria and Albert Museum (Plate 13). These tiles, measuring the usual five inches square by five-sixteenths of an inch thick, are painted in blue with incidents from the Titus Oates Plot of 1678, the pictures being copied from a pack of engraved playing cards published at the time. Examination of certain tiles believed to be of Lambeth origin suggest no great uniformity in the clays used, differing in this respect from the tiles of Bristol, Liverpool and Wednesbury where blendings of local clays were used. Lambeth used clays from various sites in the West Country.

The Bristol delft ware industry appears to have stemmed from the tin-enamelling craft founded at Brislington, three miles from Bristol, in the mid-seventeenth century. Edward Ward of Brislington founded a delft ware pottery at Temple Back, Bristol, in 1682,

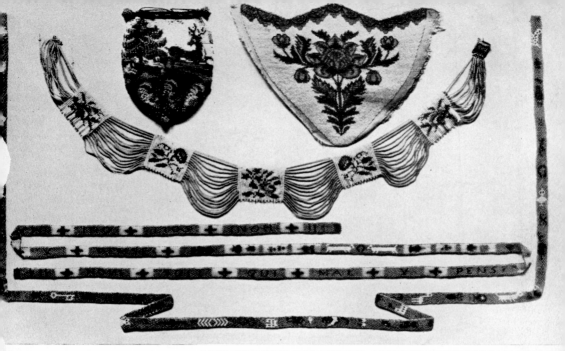

19. An eighteenth-century beadwork watch-pocket, top right, and examples of nineteenth-century bead-work. The purse carries a stag-hunting scene; the necklace has five panels of colourful flowers against white backgrounds linked by strands of pale blue beads; the watch guards below are highly individualistic, one worked with the Garter motto and the other with a wide range of unrelated motifs.

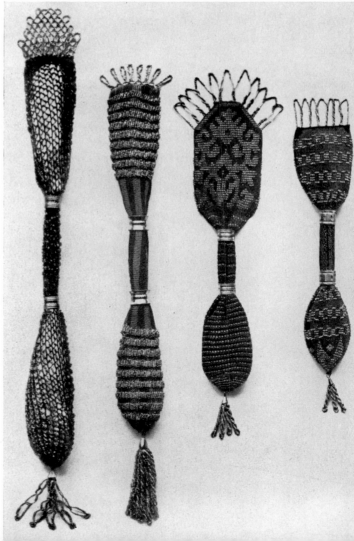

20. Stocking or miser purses of the late eighteenth and early nineteenth centuries. The coins were contained in the ends while the purse was carried by the central portion which has a slit opening: by sliding either of the rings this opening would give access to the money. *All in the Victoria and Albert Museum.*

21–24. Pewter baluster wine measures. (*Above, left*) With wedge and ball thumbpiece, a type made before about 1615, the rim struck with the crowned 'hR' excise mark and the lid with five punched housemarks. (*Above, right*) With double volute thumbpiece and *fleur de lys* lid attachment; mid-eighteenth century. (*Below, left*) With bud thumbpiece and wedge lid attachment; a short inserted strut joins the handle and body. (*Below, right*) With double volute thumbpiece and bulbous tail handle, mid-eighteenth century. *All in the Victoria and Albert Museum.*

three years before the Van Hamme patent lapsed. By the end of the century a small community of delft ware potters was operating in the Bristol district, recorded names including Thomas and Richard Frank, and Thomas Sayer. Professor Church described delft ware believed to have been made by Richard Frank as 'having a buff coloured body, harder, denser and a trifle redder and darker in tint than the body of similar Dutch wares'. Texture of the enamel on some tiles made after about 1740 suggests that one or more of the Bristol potters was using the newly improved firing kiln of the period, capable of greater temperatures than former designs.

Bristol was probably responsible for the majority of the hand-painted delft ware tiles made in England during the eighteenth century. Painting technique, generally speaking, displays the meticulous care betokening the hands of self-taught decorators, in direct contrast to the easy freedom of line shown by the Dutch artists. The colours used at Bristol were chiefly shades of cobalt blue. The blackish indigo tint dates from 1756 when English-made zaffre was first sold at Bristol and continued in use until about 1770.

The rare type of tile decorated in the *bianco-sopra-bianco* or white-over-white manner was made at Bristol and examples are attributed to the pottery established in 1743 by Joseph Flower. Against the pale blue tinge of the tin enamel, known as bleu agate ground and sometimes converted to a pale greyish hue by over-firing, were painted scrolled borders in an opaque enamel of intense whiteness made at a glass-house. In the centre might be painted a bird or other motif in colours.

Tile wall pictures were made at Lambeth and Bristol. Such pictures were composed of tiles measuring five inches square arranged as close together as possible to form a square. These were painted singly to form an all-over design and included landscapes, sea-views, formal arrangements of flowers in vases adapted from contemporary flower prints, birds, insects. In the Willett Collection was an extremely attractive tile picture painted in blue with an adaptation of Hogarth's engraving *The March to Finchley*, dated 1749. Hogarth was employed to decorate the altar pieces at St Mary Redcliff Church, Bristol, in 1745. Hugh Owen believed that Hogarth's contact with fellow-artists attending the church led to sets of these tiles being made, probably by the firm of Taylor of Redcliff Street, who are thought also to have made the set of tiles, now incomplete, painted with a view of Redcliff Church. These are in the Victoria and Albert Museum.

Tile pictures made attractive house signs and display panels for

D

business premises. In the Guildhall Museum is an example attributed to Lambeth. This is the house sign of the 'Cock and Bottle', Cannon Street, London, and shows an old English game cock with a globe and shaft bottle, enclosed in an elaborate scrollwork frame painted on tiles measuring half the normal width of five inches. One-piece tiles for setting in the chimney breast above the fireplace were made, one example in the Victoria and Albert Museum measuring thirty-eight inches wide by eight-and-a-half inches deep. Productions of perfectly flat panels of such dimensions in delft ware would offer many technical difficulties costly to overcome in the eighteenth century.

Delft ware tiles were made in Liverpool from early in Queen Anne's reign and possibly earlier. A news item in *The Post Boy*, May 23, 1710, refers to the establishment of a new pottery in Liverpool for 'fine white and painted pots and other vessels and tiles'. Some early tiles in a porous light buff clay and measuring five and a quarter inches square by three-eighths of an inch thick might have been made there. Occasional references during the next half-century show tiles to have been in production throughout the period. Existing examples appear to be the work of decorators to whom speed of production was all-important.

The application of transfer-printed decoration to delft ware tiles dates from the late 1750s. Their production in a wider variety of patterns and at less than half the price of hand-painted tiles made them formidable competitors in England and in Holland. Many authorities have stated that tiles decorated by the transfer process were first produced by John Sadler and Guy Green of Liverpool. It has not been observed previously, however, that the *Journal of the House of Commons*, November 1, 1753, records a petition by John Delamain, a delft-ware potter and tile-maker of Dublin, in which Delamain stated that he had 'purchased the Art of Printing Earthen Ware with as much Beauty, Strong Impression, and Dispatch as it can be done on paper'. Delamain was at that time also a partner in the Battersea enamel works established earlier in that year and the first firm to develop and make successful use of the transfer-printing process. It seems reasonable to conjecture that transfer-printed tiles were made at Delamain's pottery in Dublin, particularly as he withdrew from the Battersea enterprise in 1754. It is improbable that transfer-printing continued at Dublin after the death of Henry Delamain in January 1757, although his widow operated the factory with every success until her death in 1761.

Sadler and Green in Liverpool had meanwhile established a

profitable business at the 'Printed Ware Manufactory', Harrington Street, where a wide variety of tiles was produced. Transfer-printing on tiles does not appear to have been an important production until after about 1770 when Sadler retired as a wealthy man. Green then operated the factory alone until he retired in 1799. Designs were printed from copper plates upon special paper and transferred to the glaze, in various shades of black, red, brown or purple (Plates 15, 16). The black varied from a rich full colour, sometimes tinged with purple, to a greenish-grey hue brought about by inefficient firing. In some instances the transfer was over-painted in colours — yellow, blue and green in varying shades — the tile then requiring to be refired.

The demand for transfer-printed tiles appears to have increased vastly from the early 1770s. Very large numbers of delft ware tiles in the white were supplied to Green at this period by Zachariah Barnes, Old Haymarket, Liverpool. Barnes also decorated tiles by hand and his name is associated with tiles ornamented with coloured flowers, butterflies and birds.

A letter written by Guy Green to Josiah Wedgwood in 1776 records the factory prices of tiles. Green wrote: 'I sell them to the shops etc, as follows:— For black printed tiles 5/- dozen; green vase tiles 4/- dozen; figured tiles, green ground, 4/6 dozen; green figured tiles 4/- dozen; half tiles for borders 2/9 dozen; rose or spotted tiles 3/6 dozen.' The green vase tiles displayed within a scroll border a classical ewer of the type then favoured by Josiah Wedgwood and the silversmiths. These were printed in black and washed over with a transparent green glaze resembling that evolved by Wedgwood during the late 1750s. Green-figured tiles normally featured green glazed nudes and classical figures in ovals against a white ground. The figured tiles on green grounds showed similar figures printed in black line engraving, touched with stippling, left in white relief against green glaze grounds. The tiles made by Sadler and Green measure five inches square by five-sixteenths of an inch thick, edges sometimes being bevelled to enable them to be set close together in the plaster: this avoided the usual necessity for a space of one sixteenth of an inch to one eighth of an inch between each tile. Some of the transferred designs bear the signature of Sadler and Green individually suggesting that they engraved original copper plates for tile making.

Hackwood has recorded the existence of a tile-making pottery at Wednesbury, near Bilston, South Staffordshire. Here, he says, were made hand-painted enamelled tiles during the third quarter of the eighteenth century. It might be conjectured that transfer-printed tiles were made here from copper plates cut by experienced transfer-engravers associated with the enamel trade of Wednesbury and Bilston. Some coarse bodied delft tiles are also attributed to Thomas Heath of Lane Delph near Fenton in North Staffordshire.

Improvements in the composition and manufacture of earthenware ended the demand for delft ware. Transfer decorations now appeared on tiles of lead-glazed creamware. H. Boswell Lancaster refers to Wedgwood sending creamware tiles to Liverpool for printing by Guy Green, and in the British Museum are examples attributed to Leeds.

CHAPTER FIVE

Glass Beadwork

STRANGE indeed are some of the relics of the past guarded for posterity in London's Victoria and Albert Museum — and assuredly such immortality would astonish the makers. For example, there is that watch-guard pretentiously worked, twice over, with the Garter motto *Honi soit qui mal y pense* interspersed with national emblems, the whole being executed not in precious metals or jewellery, but in the naïve childhood medium of coloured glass beads.

This somewhat naïve quality of old beadwork endears it to many a collector of minor trifles. At its best, of course, it is extremely valuable, skilled work, some of it more than three hundred years old and yet as vividly coloured and clearly outlined as it was when new. Nineteenth-century beadwork necklets and wristbands, miser purses and little bags may form the basis of a collection wholly in the tradition of the beadwork caskets, pictures and modelled ornaments fashioned with equal amateur ardour in the seventeenth century and now highly valued.

Like all really satisfying form of ornament, bead embroidery was fundamentally purposeful. Not only the colours have proved enduring; the beads themselves, closely sewn over the fabric or knitted into its substance, have strengthened the cloth or leather of many an old bag, have taken the rub of wear on book-cover and casket, and have given an impressive weight and 'line' to dress and household hangings.

Venice of the thirteenth century supplied the world with great quantities of colourful glass beads made in a considerable range of shapes and sizes. Rosaries were becoming more frequently used in Christian lands; in London the makers congregated immediately outside the area occupied by the goldsmiths in Cheapside and Foster Lane — in Paternoster Row and Ave Maria Lane. In 1381 the stock of rosary beads in the possession of Adam Ledyard included blue glass and jet for the fifty small *Ave* beads, and silver gilt, coral, white and yellow ambers for the six *Paters* or gauds, and beads of white bone for children's use.

Many an Englishwoman possessed purely ornamental necklaces or 'paires of beads', by 1500, and records of a few years later described the young King Henry VIII as wearing a knee-length doublet enriched with Venice beads. In 1577 Holinshed was able to refer to such beaded apparel as a 'cloake of broched satin beded from the shoulder to the waist'.

English glassmen were making beads early in the seventeenth century. This fact requires emphasis in view of the widespread belief that manufacture began as late as Georgian days. Reference was made to them in the House of Commons during 1620, and early in the following year a subscription was opened in London for funds to make beads, not for the home market but for sale to the Indians in Virginia. In 1642 a tax was levied on glass beads, bracelets and buttons, and by 1697 John Houghton was able to report: 'In beads I am told we outdo our neighbours and are likely in a short time to serve other countries.' In 1694 no fewer than 20,855 lb. of bugles — long tubular beads — were imported into England, coming from Venice, Holland and Germany, and more than 643 gross of bead necklaces were also listed among the year's imports. But, significantly, no consignments of loose beads were mentioned, suggesting the existence of adequate home supplies.

The second half of the seventeenth century was one of the great times for bead embroidery. The collector will wisely learn its techniques and standards, and the ability to recognize the types of beads used, by inspecting authenticated specimens before acquiring examples, as much superficially similar beadwork was carried out during the middle years of the nineteenth century.

Some bead embroideries, even such sets of wall hangings as the famous examples in the collection of Earl Lytton at Knebworth, were entirely covered with beads and bugles sewn upon linen. In these hangings the flowering-tree pattern, then fashionable on Indian printed calicos, is worked in small round beads against a background of spirals or whirls composed of innumerable bugles, each measuring three-eighths of an inch long.

Pictorial panels might have bead backgrounds following the outlines of the figures, giving the work a lively mosaic quality. Even when the pattern on a bag or a bookcover was in a conventional repetitive design, the beads composing each small single-colour motif were often decoratively arranged. This peculiarly ornamental quality was something the nineteenth-century bead-workers tended to forget. But perhaps the most intriguing bead structures in the seventeenth century were the frivolous little hair ornaments, sprays and vases of flowers, baskets or open trays, even candlesticks, in which the tiny beads were threaded on stiff wires; these were built up into petals, leaves and so on in full relief supported on twisted ropes of the same material.

Open trays in this style had such relief work forming sloping sides to a central panel of wood-backed satin or linen (Plate 17). The panel usually contained one of the pictorial scenes the period loved and for which patterns were available. Solomon and the Queen of Sheba, in all the grandeur of Levantine and Carolean robes, were often expressed in flatly sewn-on beads or with some details in the padded style of the contemporary raised embroidery which some collectors now call stump-work.

Beadwork of this type appears to have continued uninterruptedly on a smaller scale until about 1760 when technical improvements in glass-making resulted in the production of smaller beads in colours more brilliant than formerly, thus starting a fresh vogue for beadwork. The almost incredible fineness of the beads enabled exquisite bead 'embroidery' to be worked in full colours. Such work dates between about 1765 and about 1795. The smallest of these beads would only fit on to special threads painted with shellac. 'Embroidery' with these microscopic beads was extremely effective, light fabric backgrounds accentuating the brilliance of their colours — red, green, and bright and pale blue predominating — in a garland of fantastic flowers, perhaps, figuring on a waistcoat in place of the conventional gold lace. Bags (Plate 18), necklaces and the like were obvious recipients of such work, which was even used for baby clothes. Design was dominated by the period's neo-classic mood, and there must have been many an inexpert worker who welcomed the straight, simple lines of the particularly popular key-pattern border, often found in blue against a cream ground.

Early in the nineteenth century glass beads were being produced in a wider range of sparkling tints and more transparent than formerly. The result was a fashion phase in which every well-dressed woman carried a handbag, made by herself, displaying colourful designs worked with beads. Tiny beads might be strung on thin silk following a sequence shown on a chart of coloured squares. These lengths of threaded beads were then crocheted with a fine hook, taking up a single bead at a time, to form elegantly graceful patterns dominated by classic themes.

Lovely jewel colours — opal, turquoise, amber — were appearing in Venetian beads by 1820 and were received enthusiastically by a period always seeking for pictorial effects. The exotic Biblical fantasies of the seventeenth century were now rivalled by finely wrought crests and monograms, by extremely naïve hunting and other sporting scenes, by views of romantic buildings, exotic birds, and even landscapes where trees, mountains and streams figured uneasily in the serried rows of beads sewn to fine canvas.

By the early 1830s the strung beads might be knitted in floral and other conventional designs, worked in transparent beads of many colours on a ground of opaque beads in a single tint. Bead-work from about 1830 included simple stringing and knitting or netting, sewing the beads to a netted ground, and loomwork which left the pattern identical on both sides. Small objects were decorated with beadwork, from spectacle cases and scent-bottles to mats and work-boxes, from wall tidies and bell-pulls to mule-tops and buttons. Trays or open baskets with sides of wire-mounted bead-mesh appeared again, and even knives and forks might have wooden hafts closely encrusted with beads on a net foundation. Whenever possible, elaborate beaded tassels completed the effect. Inevitably bead samplers were made, but these are scarce, many having been sewn on to moth-catching tammy cloth.

The stocking or miser purse (Plate 20) was a favourite form of beadwork, the beads being of coloured glass, faceted steel, or gilt metal against a textile background of blue, red or green. The miser purse was a long thin flexible bag with a central slit-opening for inserting the coins. As the purse was carried by the middle the coins fell into one of the ends, where they were secured by one of two sliding rings, usually made of silver, finely faceted steel, or gilded brass. An ornamental bead tassel on each end of the purse, one of cut steel, the other of gilded brass, or less frequently in contrasting colours of glass beads, indicated to the user which end to fill with gold coin or with copper, and which with silver. Both men and women used these stocking purses, which had a fashionable vogue at the end of the eighteenth century, and were popular from about 1820 to 1850 but continued to be carried until about 1870.

Such a purse in good condition is particularly attractive, but in general the collector of nineteenth-century beadwork searches mainly for flat handbags, necklets, wrist-bands, and the like, which testify to the period's domination by the squared simplicity and order of cross-stitch embroidery in gaudy wools on meticulously regular canvas. Even in beadwork something was lost in the nine-teenth century. There is a world of difference between a tray of the early eighteenth century and a similar article made in early Vic-torian days: as great a difference, and as notable, as, say, between Elizabethan tent-stitch and Victorian cross-stitch.

In the cross-stitch manner some of the most meticulous work

was made on bead looms: the beads were set in close rows, threaded horizontally, no silk or thread being anywhere visible. The surface of loom-woven beadwork is absolutely uniform. First, the number of beads required for a line of the pattern was counted, one extra being added to give the number of warp threads. After these had been strained over the small loom, the beads required for a single row of the pattern were placed on a weft thread and this was laid across the warp with one bead between each thread. The needle was then brought back through the row of beads, but under the warp threads. Each row was secured in this way, but the result was limited to a straight-sided flat panel, easily recognized because both sides of the work are identical, with little thread showing. The neatness, the small size of the beads and their wealth of lovely colours made this loom-work particularly attractive, achieving realistic effects of line and shading.

Small bead-woven panels on armlets and wristlets, often matching those on an accompanying necklet, might show bead patterns in naturalistic colours on a milky ground. Small as these panels are there are sometimes more than twenty shades of colour in the beads. Such beadwork was fitted with a gilded snap of the box pattern set with stones such as cairngorms or quartz crystals. Victorian taste in beadwork design ran largely to rosebuds and leaves in geometrical patterns of the Berlin wool type (Plate 19), and an occasional animal. But already another phase in the long history of bead ornament was closing. After about 1860, big coarse beads tended to reduce such work to the status of a nursery exercise.

Collectors inevitably make a careful examination of the beads from which their treasures are produced, in order to date them as closely as possible. This calls for some knowledge of the manufacturing techniques employed.

Early ornamental beads were made with the blow-pipe, and in consequence were hollow and might measure from one-third of an inch to two-and-a-half inches in diameter. The surfaces of large examples were ornamented with applied or impressed motifs, particularly foliage and flowers. In 1731 so many blown beads were made by the Venetian glassmen that eight hundred pounds of whale oil was consumed each day in their lamps. Almost a thousand craftsmen were employed in making these beads.

Hollow beads of opaque coloured glass were a much prized adornment in the late eighteenth century and until the 1850s. In London vast quantities of the smaller sizes were made less expensively than the Venetian and without the use of a blowpipe. Long lengths of coloured glass were obtained from the glass-houses. These were melted at the gas jet, the molten glass falling upon a copper wire coated with whiting. The wire was revolved thus making beads of appropriate form: the surfaces might be tooled. When cold, such beads were easily slipped from the wire.

A different method produced the beads used in beadwork. Each tiny bead was composed of a fragment cut from a glass tube drawn out while hot to a length of about one hundred feet. These tubes were cut into short rough-edged cylinders of a height equal to their diameter by means of a steel blade held in the hand and a similar tool fixed in the bench, length being regulated by a semi-circular block of metal. These small cylinders were smoothed and rounded by a firing process, but first they had to be hand-rolled in a mixture of powdered charcoal and lime to keep their holes from closing. The tubes, together with fine sand or a mixture of clay and charcoal dust, were then placed in an iron drum which was slowly rotated over a furnace. Softened by the heat, the tubes were affected by the constant friction against each other and became spherical, the clay and charcoal preventing them from adhering to each other. When cool the circular beads were sieved to remove pulverized matter, then poured into bags and shaken to remove the stoppings. Finally they were rotated in sacks of bran, to emerge with the softly lustrous sheen that gives fine old beadwork its wonderfully enduring beauty.

CHAPTER SIX

Pewter Measures

THE story of pewter wine-measures has never been fully told. Baluster measures made of lay metal are now eagerly acquired by collectors, particularly if struck with the pewterer's personal touch on the vertical rim, and with a house-sign, such as the swan and peacock, engraved on the lid. They were specially designed, at the request of the Lord Mayor of London, by the Worshipful Company of Pewterers in the reign of James I (1603–25) and were issued in an endeavour to prevent deceitful reduction of capacity by tavern keepers and others.

Until about 1612, records of the Pewterers' Company made frequent reference to 'measure pots commonly known as tavern pots'. In 1482 measure pots were noted as being in five sizes: 'gallon, potell, quarte, peingte and a half, and peingte.' A Company ordinance of 1556 required these to be of no smaller capacity than the 'standard appoynted for the same potte', which was to be kept at Pewterers' Hall for the inspection of craft members. The punishment for 'making any suche potte of less than measure' was the considerable fine of ten pounds. In default of payment the wrong-doer was sentenced to stand in the pillory on three consecutive market days. These 'standerds of the house' did not materialize until 1562, when two shillings and elevenpence was paid for pottle, quart, and pint sizes, the three together weighing 8 lb. $3\frac{1}{4}$ oz. Obviously these were for ale and beer; such wine as was drunk at this period was sold chiefly by the vintners and its consumption in taverns was negligible. In 1577 the alehouses in the County of Derby, for instance, numbered 726, the innkeepers eighteen, the vintners only seven.

At first this ordinance was used only as a threat, but in 1563 its provisions were confirmed and put into operation. This ordinance appears to have been the direct result of the fact that a certain Robert West was 'sent to the Warde for making ffalse measure potts'. His touch mark was cancelled and he was permitted to continue as a pewterer only if he registered 'Wf' as his new mark. The 'f' was indication that he had been convicted of issuing false pewter and virtually put him out of business.

These tavern measure-pots were, obviously, drinking vessels and measures combined. That they were unlidded is suggested by the piece-work price paid to the journeyman pewterer Geffery Matthews who was content to work for nine shillings per 100 tavern pots, and ten shillings per 100 stopes. Tavern measure-pots were filled to the brim; stopes were drinking vessels made slightly larger than scheduled capacity, enabling them to be lifted without danger of spilling the contents or losing the froth.

Measures for wine were also made in pewter at this period. In 1574 the Company ordered 'Roger Hawksford not to make any moe wyne pottes [wine measures] whereby to sell, of that mould or fashion, this dai shown before the maister, Wardens and assistaunces, for by their greate breadth in the mouth and shortness thereof is a manifest deceit in measure to all the queenes maisters subjects reeeyvinge wyne by the said curtailed and uniuste measure'. Spirit measures are first noted in 1612 when a comprehensive revised list of weights, numbering more than one hundred different articles of pewter then being made, laid down that one dozen must weigh one pound. No other size is listed.

Wine consumption vastly increased in England from mid-Elizabethan times. The vintner's short-measure proclivities became so ambitious and widespread that in about 1615 the Lord Mayor of London consulted the Pewterers. The result was the baluster wine-measure with the hinged lid, a more sturdy vessel than was used formerly, and designed to combat the short-measure evil. The Company laid down that these wine-measures should be made from lay metal in seven sizes: gallon, weighing 10 lb.; pottle or half-gallon, 6 lb.; quart, 3 lb.; pint, 2 lb.; half-pint, 1 lb.; quarter-pint, 8 lb. the dozen; half one-quarter pint, 4 lb. the dozen.

For centuries the Pewterers' Company recognized three types of metal: plate pewter for plates and other flat ware; trifle for drinking vessels; lay, which might contain up to twenty per cent of lead. There were, of course, numerous variations of formulae, each pewterer preparing his alloy according to the purpose and quality of of the ware being made.

Measures were produced by that branch of the hollow-ware pewterers known as potters until the early eighteenth century. The body, lid and base were cast separately and finished in the lathe; the remaining members were cast and the whole assembled by soldering. The marks left on the surface of the pewter by the tools of the old hollow-ware wheel-turners were irregularly spaced and very often in the form of a spiral. Late examples, from lathes operated by steam-power, display regular markings. The weight of the cast piece, which upon removal from the mould had a rough, frosty-looking surface, was reduced by about half by the turner. Unlike domestic pewter, the metal for measures was not required by Company edict to be hammered after casting to make its texture compact. When newly offered for sale, pewter measures were burnished to a silver lustre, but this quickly vanished in use.

Vintners, and the more prosperous tavern- and inn-keepers dealing in wines, used measure of silver, and the pewterers also met with competition from the founders and braziers, who made measures of latten and brass. Any resemblance that baluster measures might have to some leather black-jacks was merely co-incidental. The widely held view that the baluster shape was a direct evolution from the black-jack does not bear investigation.

As explained above, the pewterer assembled a measure from six cast sections: baluster body, circular base, lid, thumb-piece with hinged lid attachment, handle, and strut joining the lower part of the handle to the body. Every feature was deliberately designed to defeat the knaves inevitably to be found among so large a group of men as the public-house keepers, who numbered no fewer than 60,000 in England by the end of the seventeenth century. The new wine-measure in pewter (Plates 21–24) quickly won a reputation for accuracy and cleanliness, with the result that from the mid-seventeenth century latten and copper wine-measures were virtually outmoded for almost two centuries.

The various features were chosen so that a customer could detect by a casual glance if the measure had been manipulated against him. The gauge of the metal was required to be thick enough for the soft lay metal to defy the stresses of everyday use. The curve of the body was such that inward dents calculated to lessen the vessel's capacity were easily visible. The eighteenth-century potman was said to be valued by the ability he displayed in battering pewter tankards, every indentation giving extra profits to his employer. The curve of the pre-1680 body was, generally speaking, less bold than in baluster wine-measures made between that date and about 1825 when the slender baluster might again be found. Better to reveal dents in the measure it became customary from the mid-eighteenth century to incise upon the surface two pairs of closely placed lines cut a little above the shoulder and below the bulge. Single lines encircling top and bottom edges of the vertical rim made it apparent if the rim had been cut down in a slant from the handle.

This vertical lip rim, occupying between ten and fifteen per cent

of the vessel's total height, could not be otherwise mis-shapen to
reduce capacity without at once making the deceit visible. The
diameter of the rim and the maximum diameter of the base, which
was of a type known to contemporary pewterers as the broad bottom,
were made equal so that any attempt made by the publican to
squeeze either would distort the harmony of the vessel's shape.

The broad bottom was made without a foot-ring so that it could
be seen if the flat base were tapped up in a slight concavity, to provide short measure. The base was set in the bottom so that the
vessel stood flat upon the serving bar, and it fitted snugly against
the inward curve of the lower body ring in which it was soldered
and then trimmed to a sharp angle. Even so it was possible to reduce
capacity by squeezing base and body junction into a narrow flange,
visible because it extended slightly beyond the neck diameter, but
likely to remain undetected. The incurve of the body neck was such
that the neck diameter was smaller than the base diameter, proportions being usually about eight to five in the Company's standards.
This prevented the insertion of a false base disk which might
reduce capacity by as much as a tablespoonful.

The lid prevented a thumb from creeping over the handle and so
reducing the quantity of liquor required to fill the vessel. It was
cast, trimmed in the lathe to a true circle, and its upper and lower
surfaces made perfectly flat. The upper surface was ornamented
with one or more circles cut into it with a turning tool, and consisting of either a narrow incision cut with a sharp point or a wide
shallow gutter gouged into the metal. These circles usually included
one near the edge, another in the centre, and a third equidistant
from both. They were arranged at the discretion of the individual
pewterer, but their presence was a Company requirement.

These rings served to indicate if the lid had been tapped down
into the body of the measure. This would be virtually unnoticeable
in a flat unmarked lid, but the incised circles would become dis-
torted under such treatment and warn the purchaser of impending
deceit. The lid, hinging from the handle and resting on the rim
surface, would indicate if the lip rim had been shortened by having
a downward slope instead of closing in a perfectly horizontal position.

These features were standardized and pewterers were not allowed
to deviate from them. They were permitted, however, to use discretion in regard to handle and thumb-piece design, and only by
examining these can the collector place unmarked baluster measures
within their period.

The thumb-piece soldered to the lid by attachments extending just short of the lid's centre are found in half a dozen types in several variations. Howard Cotterell classified and named them for the convenience of collectors: wedge-shape (Plate 21), hammerhead, bud (also known as the wheat-ear or fern-frond) (Plate 23), double-volute (Plate 22), embryo shell, and ball. They appear to have been introduced on tankards in this order, and were adapted for measures. The thumb-piece, known to contemporary pewterers as a purchase or lever, usually has a slight tilt. The bud thumb-piece leans forward perceptibly, permitting the lid to be opened rather wider than was usual, giving an unobscured view of the contents. The double-volute leans backward over the handle. Some thumb-pieces give the impression of being cast in two halves and then joined; actually the 'join marks' show where the fins left by the casting mould have been trimmed.

There was little variation in handles. The early swan-neck handle was thin and light in weight, terminating in a short tail soldered directly to the greatest bulge of the body, the upper end being soldered flush against the vertical rim. By the end of the seventeenth century the curve of the handle was bolder, and was joined to the body by a short intervening strut which gradually increased in length. The tail, still plain, now curved upward and from about the mid-eighteenth century it terminated in a bulbous knob. By the mid-eighteenth century the strut was cast in a piece with the handle, with an expansive plate shaped to fit snugly against the bulge of the body to which it was soldered.

The Pewterers' Company rigidly enforced its ordinance that wine measures should comply with the standard pattern. A set of standards was kept at Pewterers' Hall for the convenience of liverymen, and complete sets of gun-metal moulds were available for the use of 'qualified masters of the craft'. Pewterers were ordered to keep strictly to the patterns so far as the body of the measure was concerned. Frequent lapses occurred, such as in 1688 when the 'Covrt condemned certaine wine measures lateley made of an unusuall forme, being wider mouthed and much deeper in the lip' than house standards. It then appeared that the house standards had vanished. The Court at once ordered that 'patterns of Samples of the ancient and usual forme of wine measures were to be provided and kept in ye Hall and marked according to ancient orders in that case made'. This new set of standards was referred to in the Company records of 1696 when the Cornish tin-mine owners endeavoured to introduce a bill to Parliament decreeing that 'no wine, beer, ale, brandy, rum or other spirits be sold by retaile in any Tavern or other Public House, but in sealed measures made of pewter'.

The wine gallon had by custom been considered to contain 231 cubic inches of liquor and the pewterers' standards had been in accordance with this. But no legal standard existed in England until 1707, when an Act was passed establishing this measurement. This standard continued until 1824 and applied also to spirits, cider, perry and oil.

Seldom are pewter baluster measures found sealed, to prove official testing. Many specimens even· lack touch-marks. These measures date mainly from the 1730s onwards, when the authority of the Pewterers' Company had begun to decline, and a considerable quantity of ware in over-leaded lay metal was issued. The wide variations of capacity noted by collectors show that the use of fraudulent measures had become widespread by the mid-eighteenth century.

Hugh Owen, when examining the old account books of Joseph Ray, a Bristol potter in business during the 1780s, discovered that inn-keepers habitually ordered their pint mugs to be made 'two tablespoons under the full' and invariably returned any of larger capacity. The Salisbury inn-keepers, it appears, preferred '$\frac{1}{2}$ pint mugs, 3 to the full pint', and from Shrewsbury came orders for 'quart mugs to hold 3 half pints each full'. Birmingham inn-keepers ordered 'pint gorges' to be made to 'Birmingham Measure', which was well below wine measure.

A law placed on the statute books in 1790 required ale and beer to be sold only from 'Winchester measures lawfully stamped'. This measure, which had been in use from the reign of Henry VII, contained 272·22 cubic inches of liquor to the gallon, slightly less than the modern imperial gallon of 277·463 cubic inches. The act of 1790 is referred to in an advertisement in the *Sheffield Register*, 1791: 'Spring Gardens, near Sheffield. Mr Rollinson presents his respectful compliments to the publicans of Sheffield and the neighbourhood, and wishes to inform those who have not yet, in compliance with a recent regulation that no beer or ale shall be sold in any other but lawful Winchester Measures, legally stamped, had their silver or plated measures which are too small, exchanged for such as is of legal size, that he repairs and enlarges old silver and plated quarts, in the neatest, completest, most expeditious and cheapest manner. He also manufactures and sells new measures.' Although this reference is to beer and ale measures and not

25. An early seventeenth-century three-legged skillet cast in bronze, its cast handle bearing the text 'Ye Wages of Sin is Death'.

26. A trivet for a barred grate, with a pierced and engraved plate of latten and a hard-wood handle. Bearing the date 1668. *Both in the Victoria and Albert Museum.*

27. A four-legged trivet described in a patent of 1767 as a 'footman to put the kettle on'. With plate and apron pierced and engraved in a design suggesting the Union of Great Britain and Ireland in 1801.

28. A curfew of latten plate, chased with two groups of St George and the Dragon and with ornamental borders in repoussé work. Charles I period. *Both in the Victoria and Albert Museum.*

to those for wine, it testifies to the prevalence of sharp practice among easily tempted potmen and the need for revision of the
law.

It was only in 1824, however, that the imperial system of weights
and measures came into operation, standardizing all measures and
making it possible for legal action to be taken against users of unjust
wine measures. Formerly the law had been too complicated to
invoke. Short-capacity baluster measures were then converted by
pewterers into imperial standard by cutting the body horizontally a
short distance above the broad bottom and inserting a section of
plate. This was soldered in position and careful inspection may be
needed to detect the almost invisible seams encircling the body.
Other pewterers less expensively increased capacity by soldering a
narrow strip of pewter to the top of the vertical rim, the lid and
hinge being removed.

Pewter measures were no longer required to follow the baluster
design, but this was continued, without a lid and with the addition
of a foot-ring. A few lidded examples with foot-rings are known
dating between 1824 and about 1830. One series of these is marked in

KENNIBURGH
raised letters beneath the cast lid & SON In some early
1826

unlidded pewter measures the hinge-lug still remains, and close
examination will usually show that the slot and peg holes on the
casting pattern have been filled with wax. Unlidded baluster
measures in the main followed the proportions originally laid down
by the Pewterers' Company.

Baluster measures made earlier than the 1730s were struck with
the maker's touch-mark on the vertical rim. The Company records
frequent admonitions to pewterers for 'striking upon his ware the
place of his abode being so much more than he registered or struck
upon the Hall plate'. The house-mark or owner's initials customarily
engraved on the lid were added after the measure had left the
pewterer's workshop. Unmarked baluster measures almost certainly
were made without complying with the Company regulations, being
either overloaded with lead or of Birmingham measure.

The theory that marks have been struck but worn away with
cleaning is untenable. Many years ago Howard Cotterell asked me to
have a steam-driven polishing mop applied to a disfigured piece of
lay metal in order to remove the touch marks, and to graduate the
polishing to the plain pewter flanking the mark, noting the time
spent. After four hours of continuous mopping by an experienced

E

woman, representing the equivalent of many centuries of daily cleaning, traces of the touch mark still remained.

From 1824 each county and borough was required to verify the capacity of all measures and drinking vessels in which liquor was sold by measure. Each was tested brim-full and then stamped with an excise mark composed of a local badge or emblem, and letters or numbers varying with the year. In 1877 the excise marks were standardized throughout the country and consisted of a royal crown accompanied by the sovereign's initials with the addition of a number representing the county or borough, and a date letter beneath. These stamps were impressed on the measure after testing by a Weights and Measures inspector of the Board of Trade.

The old English wine-measure was also the recognized wine-measure in the United States of America, Canada and Ceylon. These countries still retain this measure, thus accounting for the existence of so many unmarked pewter baluster measures. Although they were made in England, there appears to have been no obligation to strike them with a touch. Some are marked with the pewterer's name in full. Until about 1840 more English pewter was exported to the United States of America than was made by their own pewterers.

Lidded pewter measures of all sizes, particularly small-capacity pieces, have been made continually during the past half century and, apart from precise regularity in the lathe marks, it is difficult to detect suitably processed pieces from unmarked examples of the eighteenth century.

CHAPTER SEVEN

Hearthside Bygones

WRITERS have immortalized the long winter evenings spent in comfortable companionship around the old-time fireside. But they have left unsung the tedious hours of labour required to clean the complicated fireplace paraphernalia and equipment, so that the brasses shone with golden brilliance and the polished iron and steel glistened with a silvery sheen.

It cannot be emphasized too strongly to the beginner-collector of old English fireplace brassware that many of the attractive pieces displayed in secondhand shops are comparatively new. In some instances they do not even copy objects ever made in brass. The brass chestnut-roasters, toasting forks and kettle-tilting devices, for example, represent articles invariably in the old days made of wrought iron or steel, as was much of the equipment required by the cook.

The quantity of brass-ware associated with the kitchen fireplace in even large households was seldom impressive. The brassware in the 1590 inventory of Sir Thomas Ramsey, a former Lord Mayor of London, was valued at £24 0s. 3d. and consisted of '3 great brasse potts, 3 lesser brasse potts, 2 brass water chafers, 2 chafers or skillets of brasse, and a little brass morter, weying in the whole MCXXX^{11} at V^{d}p. lb^a', and 'a ewre panne of latten, a brasse panne, a latten collender, iij latten pans; one perfuming panne of latten, two great brass pannes, a skommer, and a ladle of brasse, and a small brasse kettle, weying, one with the other, cxxxv lb at V^d per lb.' There were also a copper kettle weighing 30 lb., valued at twenty shillings; three brass chafing dishes with two feet, twelve shillings; and a warming pan, two shillings.

Inventories distinguish between brass and the more costly latten. Brass was the cast alloy, usually finished by turning in the lathe and filing; latten was a soft, malleable brass hammered into hard, close-textured plates. Until about 1570 no latten had been made in England, supplies for shaping into domestic ware being imported from Germany and Flanders. Wrought goods of latten in 1545 were assessed at more than twice the value of similar domestic ware in cast brass. In 1566 rich deposits of copper were discovered in Westmorland and at the same time calamine, a zinc silicate which when heated with copper produces globules of brass, was discovered in Somerset. Battery hammers worked by water power were introduced from Germany. The alloy was cast in moulds, and the resultant ingots annealed in a charcoal fire, then beaten into plates known as latten or battery plate.

Brass almost throughout the collector's period consisted of four parts copper and six parts calamine ore; these, when subjected to furnace heat, produced five parts of brass. Not until 1738 did it become possible to make metallic zinc from calamine ore, and more than thirty years elapsed before a process was patented by which zinc and copper could be used to make brass on a commercial scale. The use of calamine ore in brass-making continued until early Victorian times, and water-powered battery hammers were not entirely superseded by rolling machines until the end of the eighteenth century.

Cauldrons, those capacious spherical boilers that bubbled upon the down hearths in the living-room-kitchens of English farmhouses and cottages from pre-medieval days, were made in bronze, cast iron, and latten and copper plates. Cooks enclosed vegetables and meat in nets which were suspended within the cauldron from small 'S' hooks hanging from the rim, a method common until recently in the Royal Navy. Boiling was far less extravagant with fuel than roasting at a down fire. A cauldron also served the purpose of a baking oven. The vessel was placed mouth downward over the bread and the embers heaped about it. Bread baked in this way was known as 'up-set bread'. In some districts the loaf was placed inside the cauldron and covered with a lid, this being known as 'pot-oven bread'.

At first cauldrons were made of cast bronze — an alloy of copper and tin — with a necked, almost spherical body supported by three long outspreading legs. The rim was fitted with a pair of vertical loops for carrying. By the mid-fourteenth century legs were made shorter. Several writers of the fourteenth century refer to the introduction of cast-iron cauldrons to the English kitchen. These were made with swing handles, and it was customary for liquids to be ladled out with a bronze ladle. Cast-iron cauldrons continued to be made with virtually no change in shape until about half a century ago.

Cauldrons were raised from English latten or battery-made copper sheets from the 1580s. The vessel was usually hammered in two parts and joined horizontally by brazing, the almost invisible seam being covered with a strengthening rib, customarily around the widest diameter of the body. Three-part cauldrons were also made. The latten cauldron was seldom fitted with legs, being made of sheets of substantial thickness and, when used with a down fire, being placed upon a brandreth — a wrought-iron ring tripod with a long handle extending from the ring into which the cauldron fitted. The strengthening rib encircling the body usually rested upon the ring. It is unlikely, owing to technical difficulties, that cauldrons of cast brass were made until the eighteenth century. Both latten and cast-brass cauldrons appear in pattern books of the 1860s.

From the cauldron developed the posnet, a small metal pot with a projecting handle, the medieval equivalent of the modern saucepan. Early posnets were of bronze or bell metal, the body being a miniature version of the cauldron, with three feet and with a flat, slightly upward-curving handle stemming from the rim. A strengthening bar extended from body to handle. Posnets were used for boiling liquids, stewing meat, and so on. Their total height seldom exceeded eight inches and they were not used among the embers of a down-hearth fire but in association with charcoal braziers, the legs holding them firmly in the glowing coals.

Posnets are known to have been in use during the thirteenth century. The Roll of Expenses by Edward I at Rhuddlan Castle, Wales, in 1281 contains an entry showing that Lady Elizabeth, the king's daughter, bought a posnet for sixpence. Inventories from the fourteenth to the seventeenth centuries make frequent reference to posnets, such as at Marketon in 1545, when a bronze posnet was valued at one shilling, and at Barnard Castle, 1680, when three brass posnets were valued at one shilling.

Silver posnets were recorded from time to time during the reign of Elizabeth I. In the inventory of the Earl of Northampton taken in 1614 is entered 'a silver posnett and cover 38 oz.'. Steele, in No. 245 of *The Tatler*, 1710, referred to 'a Silver Posnet to Butter Eggs'. In silver work the handle was usually of turned ebony. Cooks employed by the rich used silver utensils because these did not taint the food with the taste and smell of metal.

The skillet was introduced to the English kitchen early in the sixteenth century (Plate 25). This was merely a posnet with a flat-based cylindrical body and outward sloping sides, the depth being about half that of the diameter, the rim plain, the three legs short and tapering, and the tapering handle long and flat. Skillet-making became a recognized branch of the founders' craft. Body, legs and handle were cast from bronze or bell metal, interior and exterior being smoothed by turning in the lathe. A small percentage of lead added to brass improved it for working on the lathe or filing, but the practice was condemned by the Founders' Company. Hand-worked skillets of latten were made from early in the seventeenth century, but the cast variety was usual until about 1730. Both skillets and posnets were made with lids, but few complete examples remain. Palsgrave in 1540 wrote: 'He shall give a lydde or cover worthy for the skylett or lyttell panne.'

Two other types of skillet were in use, both without legs and representing a closer approach to the saucepan than any former cooking vessel. The design with a horizontal handle fitted into a wrought-iron brandreth placed in a down-hearth fire. The alternative, with bail handle, could be hung from a pot-hook above a grate fire.

The first saucepans were really small skillets with long handles in which sauce was prepared and in which small things might be boiled. They appear to have been made chiefly in silver, numerous references being noted throughout the seventeenth century and later. It is improbable that the term was used in connection with cast skillets, but it was included in a tradesman's list of latten kitchen utensils of the 1620s. These continued to be made until late in the eighteenth century, after which the majority were shaped by stamping from rolled brass.

Cookery books such as *Country Farms*, 1616, laid down that food must be put 'into a verie cleane sweet skillet', but made no mention of tinning as a protection against verdigris when cooking acidic foods. This menace to health had not been fully realized by the mid-eighteenth century, for cookery books were still instructing readers to use untinned brass and copper pans to ensure bright green vegetables. So far tinning had been impermanent, easily removed when cleaning, thus necessitating frequent re-tinning, although cookery utensil manufacturers were endeavouring to remedy this fault. An improved method of tinning was devised in 1770 by John Bootie, but the possibility of verdigris poisoning in cooking remained very real until 1790, when a patent was granted in connection with a process for preventing the corrosion of tinning and 'all those noxious effects from brass and copper when used for culinary purposes'. So impermanent was earlier tinning that any found in good condition on pre-1790 brassware must be the result of re-tinning at a later date.

Skimmers were an essential part of the equipment in the old-time kitchen, where so much food was prepared in cauldrons or open-topped pots, and spoon-meat was the main dish in the majority of households. Tusser in *Husbandry*, 1573, wrote: 'No spoone meate, no bellifull, labourers think', and Dekker a century later noted that 'spoone-meate is a messe served at Supper Time'. Skimmers were used for removing fat or other floating matter from the surface of hot liquids. Even large establishments seldom boasted more than a pair of skimmers, often inventoried under the name of scormer or scummer. The Earl of Derby's expenses for 1392 included 'ij skemours le laten iiijˢ', and the *Paston Letters* record that in 1459 there were two skimmers in the kitchen.

The skimmer was usually a disk of latten measuring about six inches in diameter, hammered into a shallow depression and perforated with small round holes. To this was riveted a long handle of wrought iron, usually flat to prevent twisting in the hand while in use, and giving an overall measurement of eighteen to twenty-four inches. The handle extended beyond the centre of the perforated brass, to which it was attached with three rivets, one at the centre and two at the rim. The other end was drawn out into a loop or pierced with a hole for hanging. From about the 1740s the disk might be made from tinned sheet-iron, but latten continued to be used until replaced by rolled and stamped brass from the 1780s.

Skimmers fitted only with small ring handles were known as flets or fleets, and were used for skimming cold liquids, such as removing cream from milk. In 1440 the fleet was defined as for 'skomyn ale or pottes, or other liquir', and in 1836 it was defined by W. D. Cooper as being used to skim milk. Only those made of latten are worth collecting.

Cooking utensils heated over a down-hearth fire were usually supported in the heart of the flames by a brandreth. When lifted from the fire the hot vessel with its boiling contents was placed on a trivet, a short-legged version of the brandreth standing at the fireside. The Maldon Court Rolls of 1416 record the purchase of iron trivets, and Caxton in his *Dialogues*, 1483, wrote of 'the ladle of the pot about the fyre; trevet for to settle it [the pot] on'. These early trivets were usually of cast iron. Not until the cost of wrought iron was drastically reduced during the sixteenth century were trivets made in any quantity by the blacksmiths. Their three legs always formed a firm base on an uneven surface such as was to be expected with the average down-hearth. From its invariable steadiness in any conditions came the phrase 'as right as a trivet'.

The trivet associated with the round-based cauldron consisted of a ring to contain its body, supported by three equidistant legs which terminated in outward extending feet plainly hammer-expanded or split and the ends shaped into toes. By the end of the sixteenth century, when flat-bottomed pots of latten and copper became more common, the open ring was covered by an ornamentally pierced plate of latten. The legs were made longer, and fitted with stretchers so arranged that they supported a plain ring upon which pewter plates were placed to warm. An example of this type in the Victoria and Albert Museum, with a pierced iron plate, measures thirteen inches in height and has bun feet.

When the coal-burning barred fire-grate came into use, the down-hearth naturally became obsolete and few examples appear to remain. The smaller, lighter trivet (Plate 26), however, was used until Victorian times, often in latten and iron, or brass alone, and provided with a handle extending outward from the front leg-ring junction. Dickens in *Oliver Twist* has one of his characters sitting 'over the fire with a saveloy and small loaf in his left hand . . . and a pewter pot on the trivet'.

The trivet-plate from the early eighteenth century might consist of a pierced sheet of latten or, more usually, a decorative open-work panel in cast brass with polished top and edges. The collector will find many of these dating from about 1820; earlier examples of this type are rarely met.

Although the word trivet suggests three legs, the name continued in connection with four-legged, hanging, and even legless stands. The four-legged trivets (Plate 27) placed in front of the barred grate and as close to it as possible were described in Patent No. 880, 1767, as 'rests or footmen to put the kettle on', the kettle later being accompanied by a dish of hot muffins. At first the footman consisted of a flat, iron plate with a front apron and supported by a pair of decorative front legs shaped from latten and terminating in bun or splay feet, and two back legs of iron rod. The legs were riveted into the corners of the plate. The ironwork on such footmen was kept 'silver-bright' by vigorous sanding. From the 1780s the plate might be of rolled brass, a type which came into general use after about 1820, when the legs might also be of brass. Dickens in *Martin Chuzzlewit*, 1844, noted the 'pot and kettle and face of brass footman' at the fireside. In the kitchen a wrought-iron four-legged trivet, among other uses, might support the dripping pan beneath the roasting spit.

The small standing trivet, with two flat vertical hooks at the rear by which it might hang from the top bar of a grate, dates from about the 1760s. The plate, in the majority of cases, was of cast brass bearing an openwork design and had two plain, straight legs at the back and a decorative brass leg at the front. Outward from the plate extended a spike fitted with a turned hardwood handle, facilitating the lifting of the hot trivet from the grate.

A trivet of this design, extending about halfway across the fire-bars, might be made entirely of wrought iron, the top plate containing openwork scrolling. From the 1820s similar, but more substantial, plates were made in malleable cast iron, always being blackleaded in use. In the kitchen such a trivet extended the width of the firebars with a plate of solid iron.

Legless firebar trivets, hooked to the top bar of the grate and extending its full width, were spacious enough to accommodate a tea-kettle and another vessel. The majority were in iron, invariably wrought until about 1820, then often in malleable castings. Examples in cast brass in a wide variety of openwork designs were made from about 1770, but are now scarce.

Heavy openwork frames of ordinary cast iron, with hooks which engaged over the top bar of the grate, were designed to extend over the whole area of burning coals, two stumpy legs resting on the fireplace back to keep the frame level and firm. These articles were known as crans, but no examples have been noted in brass.

Fender trivets in cast brass were made in many designs, basically consisting of a small circular openwork plate with a slight central depression. The plate hooked inside the fender, made stable by a flat leg extending from the outer perimeter to the lower edge of the fender. It generally supported a pottery tea-pot.

A double tripod known as the cat was an eighteenth-century form of trivet used as a plate-stand before the fire. It consisted of six legs radiating equidistantly from a central boss and so placed that it would always rest on three legs, as a cat is always said to land on its feet. The *Annual Register*, 1806, referred to a newly devised toast-stand as 'an improvement on those articles called cats or dogs, upon which things are placed before the fire'. Cats might be made of brass, wrought iron, or wood. Mrs Sherwood in her *Life*, 1847, wrote of 'an ebony cat before the fire, supporting a huge plate of toast and butter'.

Gridirons have been made in silver, brass and iron. These barred frames fitted with short legs were used for broiling over a fire and have changed little in appearance since medieval days. In 1382 Wycliff referred to 'a brasen gridiron', and a century later the *Paston Letters* record 'a gredeyren of sylver of Parysse towche, not gylt'. Silver gridirons were recorded in twelfth-century England together with glass goblets garnished with silver. Silver gridirons were preferred by the rich until the eighteenth century, and were used in association with braziers of special court charcoals. These coals were prepared from highly flexible wood and emitted an intense glowing heat until entirely consumed. Silver gridirons and braziers were used for cooking on the side-table or sideboard.

For down-hearth broiling the gridiron was of iron with a long handle enabling the cook to stand well back from the great heat. Inventories show that brass gridirons were widely used during the sixteenth century. In 1528 a brass gridiron cost one shilling in York, but later examples might be valued at as much as three shillings. These were usually square and built from cast or turned sections brazed into a frame.

Gridirons in the seventeenth century appear to have been made both round and square with flat handles. The circular type was placed upon a brandreth in a down fire or rested over the fire opening in a grate. The majority of those used with grate fires had square grids, however, and were of wrought iron with two short legs at the back and one at the centre-front beneath the handle, the number of bars varying from six to nine for domestic gridirons. The bars instead of being straight might be scrolled.

Towards the end of the eighteenth century an improved gridiron came into use. Each grille was grooved to drain into a trough at the base of the iron. Here the meat juices collected, instead of being lost in the fire, and might be poured off for gravy through a spout at one side. The two near feet were forked to fit over the top fire-bar.

Ale-warmers of copper, latten or rolled brass were most common throughout the Georgian period. They were used in the preparation of mulled ale, wine, or cider, hot drinks sweetened and spiced and sometimes thickened with the beaten yolks of eggs. The most common type of ale-warmer was a hollow cone that could be thrust point downward into the heart of a grate fire, thus heating the liquid. A long slightly rising socket handle was riveted to the rim. Another type for the grate fire consisted of a semi-circular body, with hooks for hanging so that the flat side hung flush against the fire. The mulled ale was quickly heated in this over the fire and kept at a drinkable temperature on the bars. Such an ale-warmer was fitted with a hinged lid, an outward and upward sloping socket terminating in a turned wood handle, and a cylindrical spout.

The 'boot' type of ale-warmer used on the down-hearth consisted of a cylindrical flat-based body from the side of which projected a hollow cone. This rested upon the hearth, the cone being pushed into the fire. A socket-handle was attached to the rim, in a line with the cone, and the body, lipped for pouring, might be lidded. The majority of examples now found, in both brass and copper, are of recent manufacture.

When flint and tinder were the only means of obtaining a flame to light the household fire it was customary in most homes to keep the fire burning in the down-hearth day after day, never letting it go out. There are records of fires kept continuously burning for more than a century. A regulation in force throughout most of Europe required down-hearth fires to be either covered over at night or extinguished from a certain hour, indicated by the ringing of a bell. This was to prevent the ever-present danger of conflagrations in wood and thatched structures from unattended fires. This regulation was known as the *couvre-feu*, anglicized to curfew, a term used also for the hour at which the bell was rung, for the bell itself, and for the cover placed over a fire left burning.

At first it was customary to lift the stone or cast-iron slab which lay in front of the hearth as a protective measure during daytime, placing it vertically against the fireplace recess, effectively preventing danger from flying sparks. When wrought-iron sheets could be afforded, the curfew was made from this metal in the form of a quarter-sphere with a handle extending between top and lower rims. This was placed over the embers and pushed against the fireback, thus excluding draught and retaining sparks. When the cover-fire or curfew was removed next morning, the glowing embers were sufficient to ignite fresh fuel. So far such objects have not been noted in early inventories.

Curfews were among the early articles made of English latten — they had earlier been made from hand-beaten copper plates— forming attractive objects in the hearth. All remaining curfews are in these metals, ornamented with elaborate repoussé designs. It is probable that the majority made were left either plain or decorated with simple borders of punch-work (Plate 28). Original curfews are scarce to-day. In both latten and copper they may be recognized by the mill-hammer-marks which distinguish battery plates from rolled metal.

The chronology of brass manufacture is fully dealt with in my book, *More About Collecting Antiques* (Country Life), in the chapters on Domestic Candlesticks in Brass; Warming Pans; Tea and Coffee Urns.

CHAPTER EIGHT

Earthenware Loving Cups

GREAT mazer, grace-cup, and loving-cup represent a health-drinking ritual fashionable in England from Tudor to Victorian days. *The Rites of Durham*, 1593, refers to the 'great mazer, called the Grace-cup'. This was a vessel of wine or other liquor such as hippocras, passed round after grace at the close of a meal and from which each member of the company sipped. The clumsy mazer was succeeded by the elegant grace-cup, a stemmed and covered goblet of gilded silver.

The ceremony of the grace-cup was described in the minutes of the Goldsmiths' Company after the Lord Mayor of London had dined in their hall on May 15, 1644. After grace, the upper Warden of the Company, attended by the butler, presented to the Lord Mayor a gilded grace-cup containing canary wine flavoured with lemon and sugar. The Lord Mayor 'receiving it and holding it in his hand did then and there drink. The cup then went round through both tables, passing to the left', the company standing throughout the ceremony. The butler wiped the rim of the cup after each person, and also re-filled it when required.

The awkwardness of passing such a vessel from hand to hand led to a drastic change in the design of the grace-cup during the 1660s from a stemmed goblet to a stemless covered vessel with a pair of loop handles. A napkin was passed through the loop of one handle so that each drinker might wipe the rim before handing the cup to his neighbour. The custom of grace-drinking continued throughout the eighteenth century. Prior in 1718 recorded: 'The Grace-cup serv'd, the cloth away,' and Robert Burns in a letter to Clarinda dated February 18, 1788, wrote: 'I am just going to propose your health by way of grace-drink.'

The name loving-cup for these vessels appears to date no earlier than the nineteenth century. The first reference recorded by the *Oxford English Dictionary* was found in the minutes book of the Committee for the Lord Mayor's banquet 1808. For many years it had been customary to say grace before meals, the grace-cup ceremony continuing only in an endless series of toasts. After serving the cheese the butler carried in a loving-cup of liquor which he placed before the host who filled the glass of the lady on each side from a decanter. He then rose to his feet and drank to their health and that of the whole company. This ceremony was repeated by each man seated around the table.

These grace-cups or loving-cups were in many instances of silver. The earliest post-Restoration design had a slightly tapering cylindrical body mounted on a narrow moulded foot ring, with a flat-topped single-stepped lift-off cover, and a pair of light-weight handles. By the 1690s the form had changed, the deep body with either vertical or sloping sides being hammered from a single sheet of silver plate. Early in the reign of George II, the French *rocaille* phase made its appearance, and loving-cups became magnificent examples of the silversmith's craft. The body might be chased with scrolls and flowers, and fitted with a pair of extravagantly moulded handles, the cover being surmounted by a pineapple knob, symbol of hospitality. Such a loving-cup, gilded, might cost fifty guineas. From the mid-century the incurved body in the form of an inverted pear or shallow ogee became fashionable, with a one-piece trumpet-shaped foot linked by a spool-shaped member to the base of the bowl.

The neo-classic craze brought the vase-shaped loving-cup, wide at the shoulder and tapering to a spool-shaped stem above a round foot. Handles might rise above the lid and recurve down the body. This form continued into the nineteenth century when loving-cup bodies might be spun from the plate, and there might be cast and chased image decoration applied lavishly to the body and lid.

Towards the end of the seventeenth century covered loving-cups were made in pewter, copying as closely as possible those of silver. They were also made in flint-glass, and from the 1770s in Bristol blue glass.

Between about 1740 and 1780 loving-cups were made in white salt-glazed stoneware. This earthenware was fired at a higher temperature than usual to ensure closeness of texture, making it hard as stone and impervious to fluids. It was glazed with an intensely hard film of transparent soda-glass. In their thinnest parts stoneware loving-cups are often translucent and in these interior wreathing is often present with strengthened rim and a raised rib encircling the lower exterior surface. Such wreathing is not the result of unskilful throwing, as is usually suggested. The body tended to collapse beneath its own weight while in the kiln; the slight variation in thickness prevented this.

Ceramic loving-cups were shaped on the potter's wheel from a ball of clay thrown upon the centre of the revolving block. The

potter manipulated this by a process incredibly rapid and seemingly
simple, into a hollow vessel with stem and foot. This was placed
in a heated room for a couple of days and then finished by the
turner with a few of his iron tools. He hollowed the foot, shaped
the curves and smoothed the surface. The character of the ware
enabled fine sharp turning to be carried out, resulting in a vogue
for decoration in the form of one or two groups of encircling ribs
copied from those applied to many silver loving-cups for strengthening purposes. One of these groups usually extended from either the
upper or the lower terminals of the handles. At first, handles were
shaped into loops by hand and fixed into position with slip. Later
examples were cast.

Bodies of salt-glazed loving-cups were often inscribed with simple
ornamental motifs, names and dates by means of a sharp tool before
firing. Such ornament might be emphasized with what is known
as scratch blue, by sprinkling the incisions with powdered zaffre,
the cobalt blue preparation. After firing, the line decoration appeared
in dark blue surrounded by a zone in lighter blue where the
cobalt had stained out. Some loving-cups were given a surface somewhat resembling the later *bleu de roi* of Sèvres by dipping into a
zaffre-stained slip before firing.

Numerically, however, the great period for loving-cups was the
hundred years from the 1770s, in which loving-cups were made in
earthenware. The introduction of these colourful loving-cups in
lead-glazed earthenware, at prices which placed them within the
reach of a new class of customer, dates from the period when toddy
drinking was in its infancy and hob-nobbing was fashionable. Two
friends chatting by the fireside, or in the inn parlour, would pre-
pare a loving-cup of toddy on a small table between them and word-
lessly toast each other in turn. With different sides of the decorated
bowl facing them they each automatically used a different handle,
and drank from a different part of the rim. When this custom
originated in the 1750s with silver, pewter and salt-glazed stoneware cups, it was named 'hob a nob' or 'hob and nob', later becoming
the well-known hob-nob.

Toddy was rapidly becoming a favourite drink in the early 1780s,
being then defined as 'hot grog with the addition of sugar, lemon
juice, and grated nutmeg', grog commonly being a mixture of two
parts rum and one of water. The tremendous vogue for toddy drinking during the next seventy years ensured the continuance of
hob-nobbing with its convenient loving-cups in lead-glazed earthenware. A notable collection of these, numbering almost a hundred,

has been made during the past thirty years by Mr Clifford Chubb. His collection includes a long series of specimens bearing dates, from 1784 to 1873. These are of documentary importance, displaying as they do a century of chronological improvements made by the lesser potters for sale in the Midlands and Northern England, for Mr Chubb has found only a single specimen south of Birmingham.

Earthenware loving-cups followed similar forms throughout their period of manufacture. Bowls might be urn-shaped with incurved sides, ovoid, or cup-shaped with vertical sides, the short stems thick or slender with feet domed or flat topped; or the vessels might be stemless with moulded foot-rings. They were thrown on the wheel and finished on the lathe, turners' marks still remaining. The spool stem and round foot often resemble those found on contemporary toddy rummers in flint-glass, and bowls when ovoid are approximately of the same capacity. Toddy rummers in glass, however, are found with bowls resembling nearly every form noted in earthenware loving-cups, but they are, of course, handleless.

Handles throughout invariably have their upper curves in a line with the bowl rim and extend to the point where the bowl curves inward to the base. The terminals of some early handles gradually taper to a thin edge and merge imperceptibly with the bowl. Other terminals are moulded in shallow relief, often with leaf forms. Another eighteenth-century handle design has an expansive loop, the lower terminal joining flush against the bowl at an abrupt angle and in a line with its opposite member. With ovoid bowls the lower terminals follow the curve of the bowl base. Handles may be circular, oval, or rectangular of section, usually with a smooth surface, but sometimes reeded.

Few handles have thumb lugs and rarely are these noted earlier than 1830, and only an occasional example is noted with a lower terminal scrolled. An illustration in the Leeds drawing books, however, which may be dated about 1800, illustrates an undecorated loving-cup with these features, priced at one shilling each, from which a discount of about one-third was usual.

The early loving-cups in the Chubb collection, dating before about 1815, show that the current method was to make them of soft red or buff earthenware. These were thinly coated while green (leather-hard and unfired) with white engobe consisting of white pipe-clay or local white-burning earth mixed to a creamy consistency with water. This produced a smooth, easily cleaned surface which when dry might be decorated by painting with zaffre. The piece was then dipped into liquid lead glaze and fired, resulting in a coating of brilliant transparent glaze. Only a single firing was necessary by this process. It is noticeable, however, that firecracks are frequent in loving-cups of this type, appearing chiefly on the stem or the interior of the bowl, or around the lower terminals of the handles.

Alternatively the underglaze decoration was omitted and the piece enamelled in colours over the glaze, a further firing in a muffle kiln being required to fix the decoration.

Loving-cups of engobe-coated red earthenware are almost invariably finely crazed. This network of thin, irregular lines crossing each other and resembling firecracks is due to constant changes in atmospheric conditions, the body and glaze expanding in response to these changes at differing rates. Extensive brown stains in the glaze of certain specimens show them to have experienced long periods of dampness.

The Chubb collection brings to light an interesting feature in connection with lead glaze on engobe-coated earthenware. The glaze covering the underside of the feet has invariably retained its original brilliant white condition, displaying a trace of zaffre in its composition. The remainder of the glazed surface, having been exposed to light and atmospheric pollution, is invariably discoloured, usually having changed to a greyish-brownish hue.

Decoration in blue underglaze was carried out at first by painters long experienced in ornamenting tin-glazed delft ware, the manufacture of which had been virtually abandoned in England by 1780. Attractively designed, skilfully painted pictures in the oriental style decorated loving-cups until the early 1790s (Plate 29 and 30). The zaffre used gave a rich deep blue, exceptional brilliance being produced by the use of smalt, another and more costly preparation of cobalt.

From the early 1790s engobe-coated loving-cups display evidence of speedy painting, designs being attractive but formal, and the zaffre generally of poor quality owing to war-time lack of supplies from Saxony. It is noticeable from this period that zaffre heavily applied was inclined to spread slightly on engobe made from local materials. This was overcome by preparing the engobe from the whiter-burning Cornish clays, but, with the exception of the half-dozen great master-potters, few used it for this purpose. Where the painter has accidentally overlapped two thick coatings of zaffre this has fired with a rough coarse finish, almost black in colour. This was brought about by the zaffre emerging above the surface of the transparent glaze and becoming scorched.

29–31. Examples from the Clifford Chubb collection of loving-cups. (*Top*) All inscribed with name and date painted with sprays of flowers and foliage in green, orange and blue enamels. (*Centre*) Two matching pairs: the pair with heart-shaped reserves are ornamented in blue transfer designs. (*Below*) The upper left specimen is of coarse brown earthenware coated with engobe; top upper centre is ornamented with oriental scenes in black transfer overpainted in clear reds, orange and green.

32. (*Above, left*) Musical box with dancing figures: the organ plays and the dolls pirouette. 1870s. *In the Victoria and Albert Museum.*

33. (*Above*) A cigarette-smoking monkey with musical box inside its body.

34. (*Left*) Two musical dolls given by Queen Victoria to the Duke of Windsor: the seated doll belonged to Queen Mary in the 1870s and is now in the collection of Her Majesty the Queen.

Overglaze colours in a limited range decorated loving-cups of engobe-coated earthenware and included no more than numerous shades of orange, green, blue, and black, all of them metallic oxides maturing at a low temperature. These colours, with the addition of red from about 1830, were commercial preparations widely used by the lesser earthenware potters.

A colour extensively applied on loving-cups of all groups from about 1790 was known to the contemporary enamellers as orange, but more closely resembled present-day gamboge and tan. The formula for preparing this colour has been preserved in the library of the Royal Society of Arts: (*a*) Mix together 12 parts red lead, 1 part red sulphate of iron, 4 parts oxide of antimony, 3 parts powdered flint and calcine them together without melting; (*b*) grind together $9\frac{1}{2}$ parts red lead, $5\frac{1}{2}$ parts borax, 8 parts flint-glass and add 4 parts colcothar. Grind together 1 part (*a*) with $2\frac{1}{2}$ (*b*) and store in sealed bottles. Like the other preparations of metallic oxides, when required for use it was ground with spirits of turpentine, thickened with thick oil of turpentine.

In 1764 John Greatbach, an employee of Wedgwood and Bentley at Etruria, evolved a liquid lead glaze prepared from a frit and other fusible ingredients ground to a creamy consistency in water. This gave to Wedgwood's creamware a white or cream surface harder and smoother than any glaze formerly used on earthenware. The biscuit ware was dipped in this glaze, dried in a heated room, and then fired, emerging from the kiln with a brilliant white surface ideal for enamelling. Loving-cups of white earthenware dipped into Greatbach glaze are inscribed with dates of the late 1790s.

Until about 1815 only the half-dozen or so great potters used the Greatbach glaze because the technical details involved were too complex for small rule-of-thumb plants to cope with. Exact harmony was essential between the composition of body and glaze, and firing temperatures needed to be exact. Crazing is noticeably larger than on red earthenware covered with engobe.

Until after 1815 cream-coloured earthenware appears to have been used only for the finely potted loving-cups issued by Leeds. This body followed the formula laid down by Wedgwood and was composed of equal parts of ball clay, china clay, calcined flint, and Cornish stone. Leeds loving-cups normally have bell-shaped bowls and may have either foot rings or short stems rising from domed or flat feet. A characteristic is the pair of double inter-twined flat handles, reeded on the upper surface and their terminals concealed beneath eight flat pads moulded in relief.

F

It will be noted that three firings, for biscuit, glaze and enamels, were required in the production of loving-cups made by the Greatbach process, whereas with engobe-coated earthenware decorated in blue, only one firing was necessary and materials were cheaper.

From the introduction of the orange tint in overglaze enamel great use was made of honeysuckle flowers as a decorative motif; these were simple to execute at piece-work speed. From the early 1830s there was a vogue for honeysuckle flowers in red, leaves in dark green, accompanied by bell-flowers in blue.

The rim interior of a loving-cup is nearly always encircled with a narrow border, usually composed of geometric or flower and foliage motifs. Matching motifs are often found on the upper curves of handles, and may extend towards the lower curves.

Domestic, tavern and other loving-cups were commonly painted with the owner's name, the year, and an inscription. Where these are in underglaze blue this was, obviously, the work of decorators employed in the pottery. These loving-cups were ordered from a pattern seen in the china-shop, and might take as long as three months to reach the purchaser. Enamelling of inscriptions was frequently the work of independent decorators operating muffle kilns in large towns: often such inscriptions were in a brown colour burnt in only by a baker's oven. These are recognized by the wrinkled surface of the lettering.

Loving-cups decorated with blue transfer-printing under the glaze are more frequent than hand-painted examples dating to the nineteenth century. They are seldom inscribed and dated, but when this has been done it is usually in hand-painting over the glaze. The collector must learn, therefore, to date his acquisitions by close inspection of the transfer-printing involved. This applies equally to transfer-printing on other ware.

Transfer-printing in blue under the glaze was introduced by Thomas Turner of Caughley in about 1775, appearing on loving-cups a few years later. Characteristic of Caughley transfer-printing in blue is shading in strong parallel lines as if drawn with a ruler. The technique was developed in the early 1780s by Josiah Spode who imparted greater brilliancy to his blue and used a whiter earthenware containing china clay and china stone, so far little used in the Potteries. These were finely ground with calcined flints in steam-powered mills, the first in the Potteries. They gave a hitherto unknown smoothness to the paste. The transfer was applied to the biscuit loving-cup which was then fired in a hardening kiln to fix the colour and burn away all trace of printer's oil. It was then coated with a hard transparent glaze.

The slightly smudgy effect associated with eighteenth-century blue printing was not overcome until about 1800. Engraved lines were then thinner, making tone variation possible. By combining line and stipple work on single transfers, finer tone gradations were possible from about 1810.

Underglaze transfer-printing on loving-cups was carried out solely in various shades of dark blue until 1828 when it was discovered that crushed enamel colours mixed with barbados tar could be used without distortion. Underglaze transfer-printed ware in black, green, yellow and red was then issued, and loving-cups might be decorated in two or more colours. The increased cost of applying each colour individually and giving each a separate firing appears to have limited the demand, for examples are rare. From 1848 it was possible to fix three colours, blue, red, yellow, from a single transfer with one firing, the colours maturing at the same temperature.

Spode in the 1780s decorated loving-cups by painting overglaze colour decoration over underglaze transfer-printed outlines which remained visible through the translucent enamels. Early in the nineteenth century outlines might be printed in colours incorporated in the design, eight varieties of blue, brown, and black being available. From about 1820 it became customary to leave portions of the transfer undecorated, confining brushwork to outstanding features of the design.

Loving-cups might be decorated by the bat printing process from about 1820. *The Technical Repository*, 1823, recorded a revival in bat-printing which had formerly been used on late eighteenth-century porcelain from the mid-1770s. This transfer-printing, applied over the glaze, was in black. It has been noted on loving-cups in buff engobe. Where the stippled design has worn away from the glaze light buff lines following those of the printing remain on the glaze which otherwise is discoloured, again proving adverse atmospheric effect on glaze.

Loving-cups in brilliant black-glazed red-bodied earthenware, known under the generic name of Jackfield ware, were made by John Thursfield of Benthall, Shropshire, between 1772 and 1818, but continued to be made in Staffordshire until the 1830s. These loving-cups might be ornamented with scrollwork and flowers in relief, or with oil gilding and unfired painting in colours, but seldom are more than traces of such decoration now visible.

In some earthenware designs the loving-cup contains a pair of well-modelled, naturalistically coloured frogs with wide open mouths, fixed in such a position that they appear to follow the liquor into the mouth as the cup is drained. They are usually in a light beige colour with black spots and are sometimes hollow and of a trick variety arranged to spurt a stream of liquid into the face of an unwary drinker. A loving-cup is occasionally found containing three frogs, one at the base and two climbing the sides.

Rarely is a potter's mark found on an earthenware loving-cup. In the Chubb Collection, however, there is a specimen in Leeds cream-coloured earthenware of the 1780s with the name 'Hartley' impressed on the lower curve of the body and a blue cross painted beneath the foot. The name Hartley alone is a mark hitherto unrecorded.

CHAPTER NINE

Musical Automata and Singing-Bird Boxes

AUTOMATA or animated figures are known to have been made for at least a thousand years. An illustrated manuscript in Arabic, *The Book of the Knowledge of Ingenious Geometrical Contrivances*, compiled during 1206 by Al-Jazari at the command of his sultan, describes the types of automata then known and includes several of his own construction, such as two men drinking, and a strutting peacock. The drawings show these water-driven machines to have operated on principles no different from the clockwork automata of the seventeenth century and even later.

Turret clocks are recorded as having been working in a few church towers of England by 1400, sometimes without dials but striking the hours and playing a tune every three hours. A development of the same principle is the celebrated clock outside St Dunstan's-in-the-West, Fleet Street, London, in which the quarters are struck by two figures of men wielding pole-axes. Nevertheless, automata dating earlier than 1810, when they began to be attached to musical boxes, are rarities indeed.

Until the opening of the eighteenth-century automata, with the exception of clocks, merely moved and were seldom accompanied by sound. They were usually constructed from gilded bronze. Typical was the figure of a lady dressed in bodice and farthingale carefully engraved and chased in designs resembling brocade. When wound she moved forward, turned her head from side to side as if singing, and moved her hand in such a way as to suggest that she was playing the lute she carried. At the same time tiny animated creatures were evolved, highly appreciated by those who could afford them.

In the eighteenth century automata began to be made in gold and silver encrusted with precious stones. Men skilled in producing small, intricate watch-mechanisms created gem-studded golden caterpillars that crawled naturalistically across the table; gold-enamelled mice, set with pearls and with tails of gold, that ran hither and thither at a remarkable speed, sometimes stopping to raise themselves on their hindquarters before starting to run again; jewelled frogs that croaked and jumped; and, most fascinating of all, the

85

tiny box which, at a touch on a concealed spring, released a plumaged
bird that turned and fluttered in an ecstasy of trilling song and then
as suddenly disappeared again.

Singing-bird boxes generally followed snuff-box designs, their
materials ranging from plain tortoiseshell to eighteen-carat gold
extravagantly chased, jewelled and enamelled. No technique at the
jeweller's disposal and considered capable of adding to their splen-
dour was too costly.

The trap-door which released the tiny bird, seldom exceeding
three-quarters of an inch over all, was fitted into the centre of the
top and was usually the ground for a colourful picture in enamels
such as a portrait, posy, or coat-of-arms. This panel was encircled
with pearls, diamonds or other precious stones. In the bottom of the
box beneath the mechanism was a secret compartment containing
a small golden key for winding.

In the manufacture of singing-bird boxes time did not count.
The making of a single example required the services of three
specialist groups: a master watch-maker to supply the mechanism; a
first-class goldsmith, a jeweller, and an eminent enameller; and a
bird specialist. In addition to boxes, there were also golden cages,
bracelets, cane-handles, hand-mirrors, watches, all containing singing birds. These were often given as rich presents and inscribed:
Ouvrez-moi et entendez ma voix.

The melodious song was accomplished by applying the basic
principle that a whistling note could be created by air pressure, as
first demonstrated in 300 B.C. by the engineer Philo of Byzantium.
This was applied to singing bird boxes in about 1770, a whole range
of notes being produced with a series of flutes similar to those on a
pipe organ, but other integral parts were crude. Ten years elapsed
before virtual perfection of mechanism had been attained.

The first maker of these highly developed singing birds was the
eminent Swiss watch-maker Peter Jacquet-Droz. He reduced the
mechanism to miniature proportions and replaced the series of flutes
with a single piston moving backwards and forwards in a tube.
Knowledge of Jacquet-Droz's discovery spread to other master
watch-makers, and it is known that before 1790 at least two dozen
workshops were engaged in their production.

These delicate creations are to be found in a wide variety of
detail, but there is no variation in the mechanical principle. The
bird song is generated by forcing air, by means of tiny bellows, into
a tube with a whistle outlet. In this tube operates a piston, its
motion controlled by cam wheels. These varying movements modify

and vary the tone and volume of the whistle sound. Motive power is provided by a coiled spring, the speed at which it uncoils being regulated by a governing mechanism.

The tiny bellows, less than one-inch square, is constructed on a copper-wire frame covered with fine skin of the chicken-skin variety, so prepared that it is air-tight as well as exceptionally supple. When the spring operates the bellows air is forced through the piston tube. This produces a single long-drawn note which the intricately designed mechanism converts into the characteristic extensive tone range.

The tiny bird itself contains further mechanism causing head to turn from side to side, beak to open and shut, wings and tail to flutter, and the whole body to turn from side to side. The real master stroke was to make the bird flat so that it could be concealed in a shallow box until pressure upon a tiny lever made the cover spring open. Immediately the bird rises upright it begins to sing. At the end of the song it returns into the box and the lid snaps shut. All these automatic movements were timed to a split second. Birds of the eighteenth century were enamelled and not feathered, and could not turn their heads.

Makers of singing-bird boxes were few owing to the intricacies of manufacture. Geneva was the centre of this minor art, and the public library there houses contemporary records carefully describing manufacturing methods. These jewelled toys were made by a number of London watch-makers, including a branch established in the 1780s by Peter Jacquet-Droz under the management of Jean F. Leschot, who in his turn was succeeded by Henri-Louis Mailardet. These three names, sometimes in pairs and sometimes singly, are found on singing-bird boxes issued by this firm. Makers' marks are usually stamped in the metal of the mechanism, but occasionally they are to be noted in a more conspicuous position. The majority, however, were not signed.

More specimens exist with movements bearing the initials F.R. in an oval or a diamond than any others. Such boxes were the work of Rochat et Fils, founded at Brassus, Switzerland, in 1802 before moving to Geneva in 1810, where the firm traded as Frères Rochat until 1825. Another master watch-maker who signed many singing bird boxes from about 1790 until 1818 was Jacob Frisart, who worked for a period in London.

From about 1860 a simplified mechanism was devised and less expensive singing-bird boxes made their appearance. These might be enclosed in silver-gilt or silver boxes stamped by machinery and outwardly resembling vinaigrettes. They were made until the 1930s, when they sold at fifteen guineas. At present such examples sell at about seventy-five guineas, but more exquisite specimens are infinitely more costly.

Clocks fitted with animated figures were made throughout the Georgian period, many of the world's most skilful craftsmen working in London. Christopher Pinchbeck in 1721 advertised in *Applebee's Weekly Journal* that he made 'musical Automata or Instruments of themselves to play exceeding well on the Flute, Flaggelet or Organ, Sets of Country Dances, Minuets, Jiggs and the Opera tunes or the most perfect imitation of the Aviary of Birds . . .'. It is probable that the music was provided by miniature organs, for Pinchbeck was among the celebrated organ-builders of his day.

One of England's most eminent automaton makers was James Cox, who established a workshop in Shoe Lane during 1760. He exhibited the finest of his works in Spring Gardens during 1773 and 1774, charging half-a-guinea for a view of his collection of clocks, singing birds, and mechanical toys, which were estimated to be worth £200,000. It was reported at the time that 'one of these wonders was a cage of singing birds, all of jewellers' work; their plumage is of stones variously coloured; they fluttered their wings, warbled and moved their bills to every note of the different tunes they sang which were duets and solos, supplying melodies to the universal astonishment of the auditors'.

Cox's automata were superb marvels of the jeweller-clockmaker's art, and he quickly became celebrated for his work. Within a few years the East India Company was bestowing lavish commissions upon him for gold and jewelled automata which they presented to Eastern potentates, such as the golden chariot made for the Emperor of China in 1766. A lady is seated in the chariot beneath a jewel-encrusted canopy with pendant pearls. In her left hand she holds a wheel fan, and in her right hand a tiny bird. When the mechanism is wound, the wheel fan turns, the bird flutters its wings, bells ring, and the whole chariot, apparently pushed by a coolie, moves either straight across the table or in circles. From the early 1770s Cox was working directly for the Chinese and Russian Courts, and by 1790 he had established workshops in Canton. Francis Magniac, a contemporary of Cox's, was celebrated for less lavishly jewelled but more complicated automata, a number of which were bought by the Emperor of China, including one with animated figures of parading soldiers, musicians playing, birds and animals in motion, while bells and chimes produced musical tunes.

Life-size birds in cages date from about 1790. After about 1830 the bird in a cage might be associated with a musical box, a small reed organ then supplying the notes. Usually a cage contained only a single bird capable of flapping its wings, turning its head and opening its beak. Some cages contained two or three birds of different species, each singing in turn. A change in the mechanism then caused them to chirp together.

As the century advanced the mechanism was simplified, and by about 1850 the eight cog-wheels operating the whistle had been reduced to two. These were operated directly by a spring barrel. In some examples, particularly French, the bellows might now be circular instead of square or rectangular.

Elaborate cages in both wood and metal were made in innumerable shapes. The roof was usually domed and of gilded brass bars; but towards the mid-century shaped roofs of pierced metal came into use. The cage interior was usually given a papier-mâché floor shaped and coloured to represent moss or grass-covered earth, with one or two low bushes on which the bird was perched. The mechanism was enclosed in a shallow box beneath the cage. Some cages were made with brass wire bars rising from a base of mahogany enriched with fittings of gilded metal.

A very popular series was issued from the late 1830s, the cage with gilded bars rising from a gilded base and measuring about nine inches in height. In many examples the cage was fitted with a small drawer beneath, and when this was opened the bird burst into song. Japanned cages in attractive colours with floral ornament were made in Birmingham from the late 1840s. The base to contain the mechanism was spun in a single piece and covered with thin sheet-iron, also japanned. The sides and dome were of wire fitted into three flat rings. These inexpensive cages were sold to merchants who fitted them with Continental birds and mechanisms.

Automata fitted to musical boxes capable of complicated tunes date no earlier than 1810, when David Le Coultre evolved the revolving toothed cylinder of brass fitted with projecting steel pins which worked upon a resonant metal comb. By the mid-1820s improvements had been made by which volume of sound was increased and dampers were introduced to prevent the chattering caused when a pin struck a tooth before vibration from a former action had ceased. The few musical-box automata that may be dated earlier than this period may be detected by the chattering.

The automata associated with musical boxes are usually operated from a revolving shaft upon which are mounted wheels with square cogs, cams, or pin wheels. These lift the various rods which work the figures.

Among pre-Victorian musical-box automata was the clock set in the middle of a landscape. As the hour struck horses came galloping up the road pulling a coach and disappearing behind a boulder. In other examples the clock face appeared in the centre of a sea that became a chaos of tossing waves when the chimes rang. Small figures would then rise from their seats in the rocking vessels and extend beseeching arms to the shore where windmill sails revolved. Meanwhile the musical box in the base of the clock played appro· priate music such as the overture to *Fra Diavolo*. One automaton bracket clock dating from the early 1850s was the trumpeter, already rare, although many were made. Beneath the dial were folding doors which opened at the hour revealing a trumpeter — some- times two — who came forward and played a short fanfare for each stroke of the hour, then retired into his case, the door closing behind him. In these clocks the quarters were sounded by a cuckoo who appeared through a door above the dial.

Dancing dolls were made between 1810 and 1830, but these were silent. Not until 1860 were they made in association with musical boxes. The music to which the dolls pirouette in the Victoria and Albert Museum example (Plate 32) appears to be diffused from the organ turned by a standing doll, but actually comes from a musical box concealed in the base, together with mechanism to operate the dolls. In another type the clockwork movement operates a revolving circular table upon which dance pairs of beautifully modelled dolls (Plate 38). In yet another design, four or six dolls dance in a garden to music apparently played by a violinist. In some of these an extra dancer emulates a tight-rope walker, sometimes going down on one knee. Dancing dolls were usually protected from dust by glass domes.

Dancing dolls and other musical-box automata might be set in motion by a penny-in-the-slot arrangement. In some instances the top of the box was devised as a stage upon which dolls danced and cavorted in a most lifelike manner. Theatres constructed in a similar style with larger, long-running cylinders were made during the 1890s.

The monkey series dates from the 1850s. In these, monkeys in scarlet tunics and plumed hats were popular (Plate 33). The mechanism was within the body, and when wound by a large key the monkey raised and lowered its eyelids, opened and closed its mouth, turned its head from side to side, and raised a quiz glass with one paw. In the other paw was a cigarette holder. When a lighted cigarette was placed in this, the monkey drew the smoke from the mouthpiece and exhaled it from the sides of its mouth and from its nostrils by means of a bellows worked by the clockwork. Some of these figures measure more than two feet in height and were usually modelled in papier-mâché. English examples were made by Cartwright and Evans, Wolverhampton. Monkey orchestras delighted mid-Victorians, a simian conductor leading a large group of musicians all playing with the grace of human beings. At the back, at a table on a raised dais, might stand a magician performing eight changing and disappearing tricks with cups held one in each paw. The magician was a popular automaton in his own right, and might stand on top of a mantel clock, performing at certain hours.

Other popular automata with musical-box stands include soldiers marching around the battlements of a tower, and the clown or nigger minstrel leaning against a chair and playing a banjo, beating time to the music with one foot, while head, eyes, eye-lids and lips all moved. The clown also performed acrobatic feats on the chair.

CHAPTER TEN

Flower-Encrusted China

FLOWERS were a passion with the early nineteenth-century Englishwoman. Narcissus and blue convolvulus, lily and auricula — all the decorative, lovely garden flowers — were painted on papier-mâché, embroidered on cushions, fashioned in the round in an impermanent elegance of shells and wax and feathers. But the greatest joy of every well-appointed drawing-room, fragile but fadeless, was the display of flower-encrusted ornamental china.

In the best work every petal was shaped and coloured in meticulous imitation of nature, and for technical achievement compared favourably with the hard porcelain flower-encrustations of the Continent, yet was far less costly, even when produced by such celebrated potters as the Bramelds of Rockingham, John Rose of Coalport, John Bloor of Derby, W. T. Copeland of Stoke-on-Trent, and the Chamberlains of Worcester.

Tiny moulded blossoms had been a feature of the leafy bowers called *bocages* made at Chelsea, Bow and elsewhere during the second half of the eighteenth century. But these were in soft frit porcelain. The real development of flower modelling in ceramics came in the mid-1820s, when the English potter could use to full advantage the strong, non-frit bone china introduced in the early 1790s by Josiah Spode. This splendid ware was developed by his son Josiah II who named it 'Stoke Porcelain'. Composed of Cornish stone and china clay from St Austell, crushed flints from Ramsgate, Sandwich and Shoreham, together with calcined bone-ash, the new paste eventually rivalled even the porcelain of the orient in the whiteness of its paste and the evenness of its translucency. It was less liable than the earlier frit porcelains to distort in the kiln, and preserved the sharply defined forms and outlines of delicate hand-modelling. By 1820 demand was ever-increasing and world-wide for ornamental wares of bone china richly decorated in vivid colours. In addition to the celebrated firms, at least eighteen Staffordshire potters were then specializing in the production of bone china.

Ornamental bone china encrusted with flowers modelled in the round, petal by petal, and naturalistically coloured, captured the fashionable market immediately it was introduced during the reign of George IV. It is thought that the earliest English masterpieces in this medium were made at Rockingham. Rival potters quickly entered into competition, and flower encrustation was well set for a forty-year vogue. At the Industrial Exhibition of 1862 Sir James Duke and Nephews, Hall Pottery, Burslem, displayed a group of elaborately encrusted vases considered important enough for reproduction as catalogue illustrations.

The body used for encrustation work was specially prepared as a moderately stiff paste, sufficiently plastic to adhere well to the mass. In expensive productions each flower was modelled in the round, lifelike and clear-cut. The whole range of popular garden flowers in their lovely harmonious colours enrich these ceramic confections, including dahlia, tulip, crocus, daffodil, carnation and picotee, pansy, poppy, chrysanthemum, honeysuckle, ranunculus, sweet pea. Among the most delightful are those flowers which in reality are least dependent for their beauty on subtleties of texture; the crisp petals and fascinating range of colours among the reproductions of everlasting flowers are immensely decorative on the finest pieces.

Each part of every flower — petal, leaf, stem and the rest — was modelled separately by girls on the palms of their hands, a process which impressed the paste with skin markings, still faintly visible beneath the glaze. The segments were skilfully assembled, finished with the aid of a few small wooden tools and fixed into position with a touch of slip. The completed flowers were arranged into posies and bouquets or applied singly. No two flowers were ever precisely similar, and arrangement was never duplicated; even pairs display distinct variations. In biscuit form the flowers were coated with a special glaze particularly receptive to the overglaze enamel colours which were prepared by incorporating metallic oxides with a fusible flux. Modern potters have found it impossible to equal the old modelling technique, and reproductions, therefore, are not difficult to detect.

Less expensively, tiny flowers, each pressed or stamped from a mould in a single piece in low relief, might be applied in masses. This moulded encrustation — it was no more than mass-produced sprig-work — lacks all pretence at individuality, as the process tends to flatten projections and round off petal edges.

Comparatively few pieces of flower-encrusted china are marked, and it is difficult to attribute examples to individual factories except by comparison with pieces of known origin and occasionally by the technical processes involved. Rockingham flower-encrusted china was made from a pure white paste with a hard transparent glaze, really glass composed of silica, lead oxide and potash. Where gilding was applied it might be in exquisite lace-like designs not found on the productions of other potters. The gilding is darker than that of Coalport, and with the passing of years is inclined to display a faintly coppery hue.

It is not widely realized that Rockingham china continued in manufacture until the late 1850s. In 1843 John Wager Brameld, formerly of Rockingham, established a pottery at Coburg Place, Bayswater, London. In a paste less subject to elusive shadings than any bone china yet made, but using the original Rockingham glaze, Brameld issued some impressively delicate flower-encrusted china for cabinet display.

Coalport, flourishing while Rockingham declined, issued flower-encrusted china for a further two decades. Until about 1850 this was in a hard and brilliantly white felspar china, introduced by John Rose in 1822 and the most translucent china of its period. It was less liable to fracture even than the oriental hard porcelain, a feature invaluable for thinly modelled petals and leaves. Coalport felspar body was also free from surface flaws, and was used in association with Rose's hard, white, highly lustrous leadless glaze. Gilding was light-hued and highly burnished. Such flower-encrustations are known to collectors as Colebrook Dale, a name given to the Coalport Works in 1828 by John Rose II because of Coalport's proximity to the celebrated Coalbrookdale ironworks. From the early 1850s the firm made encrusted ware in bone china.

Derby under Robert Bloor made flower-encrusted ware in bone china of rather heavy paste, lacking the translucency of Rockingham and Coalport. The glaze was usually harder and more thickly applied than that used elsewhere, and is now often crazed and discoloured. The factory closed in 1848.

The china flowers could be used by these potters to produce a limitless range of highly decorative wares, the glossy hardness of the petals mitigated by the delicacy of form and brilliant, unfading colours. They were even worn and carried as substitutes for the posies of fresh flowers that constituted a particularly endearing fashion at the beginning of Victoria's reign.

Tiny nosegays were made for sewing to ladies' dresses as ornament; others were designed for carrying in the hand. A fragment of sponge soaked in a favourite perfume found a place in a crevice designed for the purpose.

Standing bouquets of flowers, measuring from nine to twelve

inches in height, are thought to have been exclusively Derby productions (Plate 39). These were sold in pairs as mantel ornaments, the green stalks tied by pink or blue ribbons supporting a variety of herbaceous flowers naturalistically modelled and arranged against a background of foliage. In these, too, might be concealed a sponge dispelling one of the fashionable perfume essences.

Pairs of scent-bottes became fashionable during the early 1830s, heavily encrusted with sprays of flowers in high relief, and each with its gilt metal stopper surmounted by a finial in the form of an exquisitely modelled single bloom or a tiny upstanding bouquet. One bottle was intended for one of the numerous newly-invented 'artificial essences' or perfumes, the other for aromatic smelling salts. A different arrangement of flowers on each enabled the owner to differentiate immediately between them. These scent-bottles often bear a superficial resemblance to those made in Chelsea porcelain during the 1750s and 1760s, but the flowers are invariably naturalistic. Because the amount of shrinkage in the kiln was unpredictable, the lengths of a pair might vary by as much as three-eighths of an inch. Body grounds are usually white, frequently gilt with scrolling stems and lines, coloured grounds being rare.

Scent-bottles are usually pear-shaped with flattened sides, but bottle shapes are not uncommon. It is usual to give a Rockingham attribution to those of a compressed spherical form with a tall cylindrical neck, decorated with dainty flowering branches in high relief. Marked examples are known. Derby issued attractive pairs of scent-bottles modelled as a shepherd and shepherdess seated on rockwork before flowering tree-stumps. Derby was also responsible for the bottle-shaped scent-bottles with coloured grounds, apple-green being the favourite.

Coalport made a wide variety of heavily encrusted scent-bottles during the Colebrook Dale period (1828–1850) and later. An attractive series, often marked CD in blue and not known to have been made elsewhere, is vase-shaped, with foliage handles on the shoulders and scroll feet. The flower-sprays stand in relief against a white ground enriched with various insects painted in natural colours. Another series attributed to Coalport alone consists of rather large pear-shaped bottles ornamented with ascending and descending flower-sprays against a white ground enriched with gilt medallions and borders.

Pear-shaped scent-bottles ornamented with applied flower-sprays, foliage, and sea-shells, all in high relief against a green ground, were made by the Copeland firm and invariably bear the transfer-

printed mark in red or brown beneath the base. In a variant of this
theme two canaries decorate the lower body of each bottle. The gilt
stoppers are fitted with finely worked rose finials.

In a day when aromatic perfumes were essential to the art of
gracious living, pot-pourri bowls for scenting rooms made appreciated gifts. From the early 1830s the bone-china potters made fine
pot-pourri bowls in a variety of forms, the most frequent being:
(*a*) shallow, saucer like-dishes raised on three or four scroll feet;
(*b*) urn-shaped vases on short stems and domed feet; (*c*) bucket-shaped
vessels with foot-rings. These are fitted with low-domed, pierced
covers for diffusing the scent of pot-pourri. The piercings in a
variety of curved and geometrical shapes are widely spaced, or the
centre of the cover may be modelled to resemble loosely woven
wickerwork. The cover has a short central handle, from which rises
a finial in the form of a flower-spray or a single bloom such as a
rose. The field of the cover is also ornamented with flower-sprays
in relief, and its rim may be enriched with scrollwork in burnished
gold. The exterior of the saucer-shaped vessel is undecorated except
for the gilded rim. Deep bowls were enamelled with flowers
enclosed in gilded cartouches on a coloured ground. Oval containers
moulded to resemble basket-work have rims and covers flower-
encrusted.

Rockingham, Coalport and Derby all made pot-pourri bowls of
these types: the two latter firms, and John Davenport of Longport,
from about 1840, also issued rectangular bowls with gilt scroll or
foliage handles on the narrow ends and with four shell feet. The
pierced covers are heavily encrusted and the exteriors painted with
flower-sprays in coloured or gilded cartouches. Bloor of Derby,
Copeland and others issued miniature pot-pourri bowls in the form
of circular baskets measuring two and a half to three and a half
inches in diameter, raised on three or four gilded ball-and-claw feet,
their exteriors ornamented with bouquets and sprays of flowers in
high relief, sometimes with the addition of fruit. Copeland made
similar bowls decorated with birds in the round; these bear a transfer mark in brown or red.

In very many instances, however, the flowers were mounted and
presented entirely as ornamental pieces. These included the vases
of vividly coloured flowers arranged as pyramidal bouquets. Such
vases are usually of urn form, sometimes with turned-over lips,
elaborated with rococo scroll and wave ornament. Bases may be
square, but later they were circular and domed, often with scalloped
rims. Front and back of such a vase display splendidly painted

35. (*Above*) A singing bird musical box with a cage of fretwork and gilded brass wire, containing canaries that move and sing. 1840s.
36. (*Above, right*) A singing bird in gold filigree cage with blue enamel Corinthian columns. About 1800. *By courtesy of Messrs Christie, Manson & Woods Ltd.*
37. (*Below*) A small singing bird box: the mechanism operates a secret compartment which flies open to reveal a portrait. *In the collection of Mr Roland Winder.*
38. (*Below, right*) Bavarian dancing dolls with musical box: the three couples are attached to a revolving disk and each also pirouettes on a central stem. 1870s.

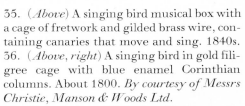

39. (*Above, left*) One of a pair of Derby standing bouquets of flowers. *By courtesy of Messrs Christie, Manson & Woods Ltd.*

40. (*Above*) A Colebrook Dale flower-encrusted clock case containing an eight-day fusee and chain clock by Vulliamy of London. *By courtesy of Mr T. Leonard Crow.*

41. (*Centre, left*) A pair of Derby peacocks with plumage in colour and gold, perched on flowering tree-stumps: modelled by J. J. Spengler after a design by Angelica Kauffmann. *In the Wernher Collection.*

42. (*Left*) A Colebrook Dale dish of flowers and fruit, finely modelled in full relief and decorated in natural colours. *By courtesy of Messrs Christie, Manson & Woods Ltd.*

panels of flower-sprays in full colour, or exotic birds in landscapes. Occasionally such a pair might be centred by a triple flower vase.

Derby made vases of garden flowers bearing pairs of gilt masks or scroll foliage handles, with claw and shell feet. Front and back are panelled with flower-encrustations against white or coloured grounds. Small basket-shaped vases of flowers, no more than four inches across, are found with the Coalport pseudo-Dresden mark in blue.

Dishes bearing superbly modelled garden flowers, of full size and in their natural colours, made handsome decorations on early- and mid-Victorian dining tables (Plate 42). The fashion for such flower decoration dates to little earlier than Victorian days. Few homes could obtain real flowers during the winter months, hence the popularity of everlasting flowers. It is probable that Rockingham was first in the field with these gorgeous table pieces, the last word in fine modelling, harmonious colours, and artistic arrangement. Coalport was more prolific in its output.

These dishes are most usually modelled to represent oval or circular wicker-work baskets in cane-yellow. The larger specimens may have entwined or interlaced hoop handles in green, which may be pierced; smaller ones have pairs of interlaced scroll or D handles. A series marked with the old Derby crown and D with batons and dots flanked by the letters S & H were made by Stevenson and Hancock of Derby from 1860. From about 1865 the batons were replaced by swords with hilts.

Other specimens of equally superb quality represent plates of flowers and fruits similarly modelled full size and in their natural colours. These, in their way, are small masterpieces of ceramic art, the English bone-china specimens often being superior to the products of Dresden. Some stand on four partly gilt scroll feet, their rims shaped with scrolls and decorated with low-relief, gilded trellis-work. In those made at Coalport, which might bear a pseudo-Dresden mark in blue, there was apparently some difficulty in firing the larger plates, ten inches and more in diameter, with their flowers and fruits, for faint fissures beneath, produced in the kiln, are found concealed under heavily enamelled insects and detached flower sprays such as forget-me-nots. Rockingham made a series with a leaf-shape plate about four and a half inches wide displaying a variety of beautifully modelled flowers.

At the same time, another type of basket was produced in which the flowers merely rimmed the oval, loop-handled vessel. This was a favourite ornament with early Victorians. The majority display

G

evidence of speedy workmanship, but early models were cabinet
pieces, exquisitely encrusted and lavishly enriched with highly
burnished gilding. Such baskets may measure between seven and
fifteen inches in length. Rims are usually waved and encircled with
hand-modelled flowers, often in association with trailing foliage.
In fine examples these are exquisitely modelled; less fragile are the
more frequent moulded flowers. The junctions of handle and body
may each be concealed beneath an expansive blossom, shell
medallions in this position dating from the mid-1840s. The base
may lie flat upon the table, but more usually it is raised upon four
gilded scroll feet or on a modelled spreading foot rim enlivened with
touches of gilding.

The sides of the basket interior are painted with bouquets and
flower-sprays encircled with gilded scrollwork. The exterior is
usually white, forming a ground for cleverly arranged flowering
stems in full relief, or for bouquets and detached sprays in vivid
colouring. Less frequently the ground may be laid with light blue,
royal blue, bright periwinkle-blue, apple-green, lilac, yellow, or
pink made resplendent with gilding.

Rockingham issued closely encrusted baskets woven from straws
of bone china and coloured white, off-white, or cane-yellow. From
Coalport came the oval basket in cane-yellow moulded in the form
of interlaced wickerwork, the interior base ornamented with a pair
of pheasants and a landscape.

A more spectacular Coalport production, combining flower encrustation and printed ornament, is the series of spherical, lidded bowls,
measuring ten to twelve inches in diameter and seven to nine inches
in height, with green entwined rustic D-shaped handles. The front
of such a bowl is painted with a pictorial scene such as a country
mansion set in elaborate gardens, while the reverse displays either a
matching scene or a bouquet of flowers. The scenes are named in
gold around the foot rim, such as 'Warwick Castle' and 'Cottage at
Battle Bridge'. Flower-encrustations flank each painting, four
groups in all. The slightly domed cover has a flower-spray finial
encircled with encrusted flowers.

Vases in pairs and sets of three were issued in a wide range of
forms, the quality of the flower-encrustations varying from the
finely hand-modelled to rather crude moulding that lacks even hand-
finishing. Coalport was responsible for a remarkable series of baluster vases, square on plan with pierced and waved lips, supported
on square cushion-bases decorated to resemble black-veined marble.
To the exterior of each vase are applied exotic birds with nests of

eggs and a cupid among exotic flowers, against a white ground painted with fruit, insects, flower posies and foliage. Coalport also made flower-encrusted vases with high scroll handles connecting lip to shoulder, and the ground painted with flowers and insects.

Bottle-shaped vases of the globe-and-shaft type measuring twelve to sixteen inches in diameter were made by several Staffordshire potters from the mid-1840s to the early 1860s. These may be encrusted all over with detached flower-sprays in colour, gilt-enriched. Others bear spirals of flowers extending from foot to mouth rim.

Chamberlains of Worcester made some exceptionally elaborate encrusted vases with covers. These were built in three parts: (*a*) a tall, spreading, pedestal foot with a scalloped rim; (*b*) a body, oval on plan, with vertical loop handles rising from the shoulders; (*c*) a highly domed cover with scrolled rim surmounted by a tall pinnacle flower-cluster. Stem and body are firmly joined by a metal bolt. These vases are elaborately modelled with pendant flowers in high relief on the shoulders, and usually bear the Chamberlain mark in the lid.

Encrusted standishes and inkstands found a place in every fashionable drawing-room during the 1840s and remained a popular ornament for another quarter of a century. A flat standish tray with a narrow, dished depression for pens, or sometimes raised on three or four scroll feet, carries a beaker or vase-shaped inkwell and shot-container flanking a taperstick or wafer-box. Each container may be modelled in the form of a blossom; others have covers modelled as roses with butterfly finials.

Encrusted trays, each containing a single ink-vase with a domed cover supporting a small, delicately modelled bouquet finial, were made by Coalport and Derby, and from the late 1840s by several Staffordshire potters. In another form the ink-vase was hand-modelled as a carnation rising from a shaped, flower-encrusted dish. For the desk, also, were Coalport's paperweights. One rare type shows the moulded figures of a girl and youth reclining on flower-encrusted rockwork.

Encrusted figures and statuettes displaying a notable palette of brilliant and delicate colour were made at this period, particularly desirable being the pairs of peacocks made at Derby in the late 1830s and later (Plate 41). These represent peacocks with plumage radiant in colours and gold, perched on flowering tree-stumps rising from oval bases. They were copied from the model made by John James Spengler half a century earlier after a design by Angelica Kauffmann.

The vogue for encrusted china brought with it a genteel demand for the most unlikely dust-catching trifles in this medium. Fragile wall-pockets, with back-plates modelled as open yellow wickerwork with a rope-pattern border, were interlaced with flowering branches in natural colours. These were made by Coalport, and from the late 1840s by several Staffordshire potters. Rockingham issued a series of splendid wall plaques, many of which have been preserved only because framed and glazed. In these, bouquets of brilliant flowers such as tulips, dahlias, primulas, roses, and other garden favourites are handsomely displayed against highly glazed white grounds.

The collector of flower-encrusted china will find no end to the objects enriched in this way, from candelabra and tapersticks to cabinet cups, saucers, and ewers, from cottage pastille burners and night-lights to the merest candle-snuffer.

Index